EMLYN HUGHES
A TRIBUTE TO CRAZY HORSE

PHIL THOMPSON

Dedicated to Brian Thompson

First published 2006

STADIA is an imprint of
Tempus Publishing Limited
The Mill, Brimscombe Port,
Stroud, Gloucestershire, GL5 2QG
www.tempus-publishing.com

© Phil Thompson, 2006

The right of Phil Thompson to be identified as the Author
of this work has been asserted in accordance with the
Copyrights, Designs and Patents Act 1988.

British Library Cataloguing in Publication Data.
A catalogue record for this book is available from the British Library.

ISBN 0 7524 3953 7

Typesetting and origination by Tempus Publishing Limited
Printed in Great Britain

EMLYN HUGHES

A TRIBUTE TO CRAZY HORSE

CONTENTS

CHAPTER 1

'If this boy was as good at football as he thinks he is, he would play for England' – Emlyn Hughes' school report, 1958

Emlyn Walter Hughes was born in the Cumbrian town of Barrow-in-Furness on 28 August 1947. Emlyn's father, Fred 'Ginger' Hughes, had represented Great Britain at rugby league after moving to Barrow to join the local rugby league club. Fred came from Llanelli and had played for Wales Schoolboys as a youngster, and when an invitation came for him to play professional rugby league for Barrow for a signing-on fee of £500, he moved to Cumbria. His original plan was to take the £500 and then return to Llanelli as soon as possible. Fred told his brothers Harry, Dick and Emlyn (Emlyn Hughes was named after his uncle) that he had no qualms about signing for Barrow, but he would be returning home to the Welsh valleys before too long. The Hughes family consisted of seven children and Fred was often the only one bringing in a regular pay packet. No doubt a large chunk of the £500 found its way back to Llanelli, but Fred Hughes immediately took a liking to life in Barrow and decided to honour his contract and stay.

Playing as a prop forward for Barrow, he soon became a popular figure at their home ground, Craven Park. After a successful career at Barrow, he signed for Workington and played alongside the famous Gus Risman, at the time known as one of the hardest men in rugby league. Fred Hughes thought his rugby days had come to an end after retiring when Workington released him. An offer then came out of the blue for Fred to represent Wales against England in a rugby league international. He hadn't played at all for two years, but, after a great deal of persuasion from Gus Lisman, he put his boots on again to represent his country against the old enemy.

When his rugby days finally came to an end, Fred was involved in a variety of occupations before setting up a tarmacking business with a friend. He even tried his hand at being an on-course bookmaker at the Westmorland course at Cartmel. Fred took the bets, Emlyn's mother Anne, as clerk, did the paperwork and Fred's brother Dick was the tic-tac man in the ring. Fred Hughes was never a licensed bookmaker, but the authorities never bothered him as he set up his pitch at Cartmel for a number of years. His pitch was known on the course as 'Ginger's Hill'. He was happy to make a profit of £20 and would not take a chance on laying big bets.

Cartmel races was a day out for the whole of the Hughes family and Emlyn Hughes' own love of horse racing originated from his childhood days accompanying his family on their annual visit to the beautiful Westmorland course. In later years, Emlyn Hughes became a racehorse owner and even had a runner in the Grand National during the 1970s.

Fred Hughes' tarmac business continued to put food on the table and he was happy to remain in Barrow with his wife Anne and their three boys, David, Emlyn and Gareth. David was four years older than Emlyn, with Gareth the youngest. Emlyn was born at 94 Blake Street in August 1947. Although the main source of employment in Barrow-in-Furness was shipbuilding, Fred Hughes was far too independent to have sought work at the local shipyard when his rugby days came to a close. Running his tarmac business suited him down to the ground. Most people in Barrow knew Fred Hughes as he walked through the town centre proudly wearing his British Lions blazer everywhere he went.

Although Fred Hughes was a confirmed rugby fanatic, he encouraged his children to be the best they possibly could in whatever was the sport of their choice. When Fred noticed that young Emlyn looked quite a prospect at football, that was it – from that moment on Fred attended every game, work commitments permitting, that he possibly could. Even if his son had a bad game Fred would be there after the match telling him that he was by far the best player on the pitch. If

Emlyn Hughes did not succeed in becoming a professional footballer it would not be through a lack of confidence in his own ability – Fred 'Ginger' Hughes saw to that.

The family moved from Blake Street to a place just outside the town centre named Abbots Vale. Their new home was Vale Cottage, a bigger abode with a driveway where the growing Emlyn Hughes could hone his blossoming football skills. As soon as he got home from his local school, South Newbarns Juniors, it was England against Wales with his brothers and pals in the driveway. Young Emlyn was always on the England side, his ambition, even at an early age, being to play for the country of his birth and not his parents' homeland of Wales.

Apart from his father, Emlyn Hughes stated in his autobiography that it was at South Newbarns Junior School that he came under the guidance of another influential figure in his young days as a footballer. Joe Humphreys was the headmaster of South Newbarns and took the under-11 football team. Emlyn's school was the top team in Barrow for that age group during his days at the school. Some hard games took place against other local schools, but South Newbarns generally came out on top.

It was also during this period that Emlyn Hughes started to make regular visits to Holker Street to watch his idols Barrow Football Club take on the likes of Accrington Stanley and Workington Town in the old Third Division (North). Fred Hughes had always hoped that Emlyn might take a shine to rugby league as his sport of choice but, although Emlyn tried the oval ball game, he soon realised that it was football and not rugby where his talents lay.

The young Emlyn Hughes became so obsessed with Barrow FC that he even took to travelling to away games, as far afield as the likes of Exeter City, when the mood took him. If he didn't have the money, he would hitchhike to away games with his younger brother Gareth. When the two dishevelled and hungry youths arrived back home they would inevitably receive a telling-off from their relieved parents before sports-mad Fred Hughes would then write a note excusing them for any absence from school.

Going on to secondary school, Emlyn continued to shine at sport at Risedale Secondary Modern. He played rugby league as well as football for the school and was selected to represent Barrow at rugby. The opposition were St Helens, who as always were full of talented young rugby league prospects. Barrow were thrashed 47-0, and this confirmed in young Emlyn's mind, and that of his father Fred, that the round ball game was where his future might lie.

CHAPTER 2

'They called me The Underseal Kid because that's all I could do' – Emlyn
Hughes recalling his days as an apprentice motor mechanic.

At Risedale Secondary Modern, Emlyn Hughes represented the
school at cross country running as well as football and rugby. At the
age of thirteen, however, his spurt of growth came to a temporary
end. The other lads in the school caught up with him and in many
cases overtook him when it came to size and physique. From being
the outstanding young sportsman for his age group, his peers now
overtook him as they grew stronger.

His interest in playing football received a temporary setback, but
his allegiance to his heroes in the blue and white of Barrow Football
Club remained as strong as ever. He even approached the club secre-
tary at Holker Street one day to request a trial for Barrow. The club
allowed him to train with the amateurs and youth team players of an
evening when he reached the age of fifteen. At this period in his teenage years, however, Emlyn Hughes was not the young strapping hulk
of a teenager who would impress Bill Shankly when the legendary
manager witnessed his Blackpool debut four years later. Barrow failed
to take him on, mainly on the grounds that he wasn't big enough for
the tough, hard world of Fourth Division football.

At this stage Fred Hughes' tarmac business was beginning to develop
and Emlyn was packed off to learn a trade. Fred's choice was that he
should be a motor mechanic and his dejected young son began work as
an apprentice at a firm situated in Barrow, aptly named Emlyn Street.

Emlyn Hughes hated his days working in the garage, his dream still
being to become a professional footballer. However, he reasoned that

if he hadn't shown enough promise for Barrow to take him on, then he had very little chance of impressing a bigger club.

Emlyn continued to play local junior football in the Barrow and District League. The club he signed for was Roose Juniors. There he came under the guidance of Bill Evans, who instilled in Hughes a new determination to make it in football, but it was through the sheer determination of Fred Hughes that the crucial breakthrough came.

Emlyn continued to play for Roose on Saturday and Sunday after-noons, while Fred Hughes worked behind the scenes to get his son a trial at a professional club. If anyone wants to know from whence Emlyn Hughes got the incredible drive and determination that was such a feature of his fantastic football career, they need look no further than his father Fred Hughes. Although Fred would have loved to have seen Emlyn become a top rugby league player, like his eldest son David did at Barrow, he never gave up helping his football-obsessed offspring to fulfil his dream.

Emlyn continued to set off every morning to the garage in Emlyn Street to learn the ins and outs of becoming a motor mechanic. In later years he confessed that the only job he was any good at when it came to car repairs was undersealing them. 'They called me The Underseal Kid,' he once exclaimed, 'because that was all I could do.'

Emlyn Hughes' parents were no different from any others during the 1960s in wanting their children to learn a trade as the passport to happiness and a means of earning a living. Like a great number of teenagers forced into embarking on five-year apprenticeships that would 'set them up' in later life, Emlyn Hughes resented every minute of it.

He played his heart out every weekend for Roose Juniors, hoping that a scout from one of the Lancashire clubs might be standing on the touchline and be suitably impressed with his all-action style of play. At this stage in his career, Emlyn was still playing as an inside forward, and scored his fair share of goals. He once set a record for goalscoring during his days playing for South Newbarns under-11s and he always thought his future in the game would be as a forward.

The big break for Emlyn Hughes came when his father decided to approach Ron Suart, the Blackpool manager, in the hope of attaining a trial for his son at Bloomfield Road. Emlyn knew that Suart was a native of Barrow and Fred Hughes had known the likeable Suart for many years. Suart had been a top defender for Blackpool and Blackburn Rovers during his playing days and after winning promotion to the Second Division for Scunthorpe in 1958, it was clear he was an up-and-coming young manager.

Blackpool offered Ron Suart the opportunity to become a First Division manager at the beginning of the 1958/59 season and he took over the reins at Bloomfield Road. Suart was known as an honest manager and was very quietly spoken. He had developed a reputation for bringing young talent to fruition at Blackpool and one only has to look at the careers of two future England greats, Alan Ball and Emlyn Hughes, to realise that his ability to spot young talent was second to none.

After months of badgering by his persistent son, Fred Hughes took the opportunity, while carrying out some tarmac work in Blackpool one day, to make his way to Ron Suart's office and attempt to get Emlyn a trial at the club. With Suart being a Barrow-born man, surely, he thought, he would give a talented kid from his own place of birth just one chance to show his worth.

Fred's determination paid off and he was invited to bring his son to Bloomfield Road the following week. Emlyn Hughes was ecstatic. He always had confidence in his own ability and now he had a chance to prove himself at a First Division club. The problem was, however, that Emlyn Hughes had still not undergone that spurt of growth that made him look such a powerful player in later years. He was still relatively small for his age and although Blackpool's assistant manager Eric Hayward and youth team coach Bobby Finnan thought Emlyn Hughes had ability, his size went against him. After running the rule over Emlyn in a few trial games, they told Fred to bring his son back in a few months. Fred and Anne Hughes then set about building up their growing teenage son with a diet of steaks and whatever else they could feed him up on.

Emlyn Hughes started to play the occasional game for Blackpool's 'B' team and assistant manager Eric Hayward began to take a keen interest in the youngster's performances. Hayward had been a centre half in the famous Blackpool glory days of the mid-1950s when the seasiders had won the FA Cup in a fabulous 1953 final against Bolton.

Blackpool manager Ron Suart, the man who gave Emlyn Hughes his first break
in professional football. Suart told Emlyn after his debut against Blackburn, during
which he attempted to kick everyone in a blue and white shirt, 'You certainly made
an impact out there son.'

He knew the game inside out and began to give the young Emlyn Hughes a rollicking on a regular basis. Hughes was at first disconcerted to be on the receiving end of Hayward's tongue lashings, but then reasoned that if he didn't have anything to offer then the old pro wouldn't have bothered with him. Hayward cajoled Hughes with a mixture of bullying and praise into becoming a better player. Added to the fact that he was now beginning to grow much bigger and stronger, Emlyn Hughes was now starting to look a prospect. If Ron Suart or Eric Hayward turned up to take a look at training sessions or junior team matches that Hughes was involved in, the youngster from Barrow pulled out all the stops in an effort to impress them.

As at every stage of his son's development, Fred Hughes now decided to make the next move in Emlyn Hughes' career. He moved Emlyn out of the family home and set him up in digs in Blackpool. He wanted him nearer to the training ground at Squires Gate and he also contacted a garage to enable him to continue his apprenticeship as a motor mechanic. Although he was reluctant to leave the warmth of the family home in Barrow, Emlyn Hughes knew he had to give football his total commitment if he was ever to fulfil his dream of becoming a professional. Emlyn Hughes lodged at 2 Levens Grove, Blackpool with Johnny Green, Hughie Fisher and Alan Ball. Green and Fisher would eventually become top-class First Division players; Hughes and Ball were destined to become football legends. At some stage in the future a blue plaque should be erected at 2 Levens Grove stating that it was once the residence of two future England captains.

Emlyn Hughes settled in well at his new lodgings and was well looked after by his landlady Mrs Mawson. He would work in the day at Blackpool's Imperial Garage and then make his way to Squires Gate for training sessions in the evening. He envied his fellow lodgers at Levens Grove who would still be in bed when he was setting off for work on a cold winter's morning. Emlyn would have to do a full day's work and grab a quick bite to eat during the day before setting off for training at 5.00 p.m. The full-time apprentices were allowed to concentrate fully on their football careers at Blackpool. Hughes would arrive back at his digs to eat his evening meal often after nine at night. It was all worth it to Emlyn, however; he had always wanted to be a part of a top First Division club and he was now well on the way to achieving his dream.

Now playing in midfield, Emlyn Hughes eventually forced his way into the Blackpool youth team. He really made his mark when he knocked a goal in past Blackpool's star goalkeeper, Tony Waiters, in a pre-season trial match playing for The Whites against The Tangerines. These public trial games were a feature of most teams' pre-season activities at the time and would allow the supporters a taste of what would be on offer in the coming season.

Hughes was now beginning to make his mark at Blackpool and had even received a mention in the local press. Fred Hughes told Emlyn that Ron Suart had assured him that the teenager was soon to be offered professional terms at the club. He had been training at Blackpool for a year and a half and the day arrived when he was called into Suart's office to hear whether or not he was to be offered a contract. When Suart told him the magic words – that he was to become a full-time professional – Hughes could not contain his joy. He felt as though he was walking on air as he quickly signed the form put before him and left Suart's office. The fact that he would now be receiving the princely sum of £8 a week didn't concern him in the slightest. He could now train full time and his dreaded days as an apprentice motor mechanic were destined to become a rapidly fading memory.

CHAPTER 3

'At Blackpool I remember Emlyn Hughes telling me that I'd always be a banker, or something that sounded very similar' – Graham Kelly, former chief executive at the FA and a teammate of Emlyn Hughes as a youngster at Blackpool.

Blackpool FC, the club Emlyn Hughes became a full-time professional with in 1964, was a club in decline. The only trophies they had ever won were the Second Division Championship in 1930 and the FA Cup in 1953. They had finished runners-up to Manchester United in the First Division in 1956, but had been 11 points behind the brilliant 'Busby Babes'.

Despite the fact that they were now struggling to maintain their First Division status, there was still something special about the seaside club. Perhaps it was the almost exotic tangerine shirts that they played in, or the memories of the great Stanley Matthews leading a sensational Blackpool fightback against Bolton Wanderers in the FA Cup final of 1953.

Despite their lack of success when it came to silverware, Blackpool had always produced outstanding players throughout their history. From Jimmy Hampson in the 1930s and the great Stan Mortenson in the post-war period through to Jimmy Armfield, Gordon West and Alan Ball in later years. The production line of top professionals kept rolling on.

Although they regularly had gates of 30,000-plus in the 1940s and '50s, by the 1960s attendances had fallen and, to survive, Blackpool had to sell their best players when suitable offers came along. Apart from the outstanding England full-back Jimmy Armfield, who made 568 appearances for the club, most of their top players moved on when a bigger club came in for them.

Emlyn Hughes admitted that his first year as a full-time professional at Blackpool did not go as well as he expected. Training with
the likes of Armfield, Ball, Waiters, Green and all the other first-team
players helped to bring him on, but he still thought a breakthrough
into the First XI was years away. He turned out for the 'A' and 'B'
teams on a regular basis, but his aim was to make an appearance for
the Central League side. The Central League was the last step before
the first team and Emlyn Hughes was in a hurry to make the next
step up in his career.

Although Alan Ball shared the same lodgings as Emlyn Hughes, he
was spending less and less time at Levens Grove. His parents lived in
Farnworth, which was a short distance from Blackpool. Ball would
spend only a couple of evenings a week at his lodging house, but
Emlyn Hughes was taken for a drive around Blackpool by the future
England World Cup hero on the odd occasion. Alan Ball had a red Ford
Zephyr and the youngsters at Mrs Mawson's found it a great thrill to
be seen parading around Blackpool town centre with the local football
club's up-and-coming star.

Emlyn Hughes might have looked up to Ball as a player, but that
didn't stop him once getting stuck into him with a piledriver of
a tackle that would become his trademark in later years. During a
practice session at Squires Gate, Hughes left Blackpool's prized asset
writhing on the ground in agony after hitting Ball just above the
ankle in a full-blooded attempt to take possession of the ball. The
Blackpool training staff gave Hughes a rollicking as they attended to
the stricken Ball.

When the game restarted Alan Ball noticed that Emlyn Hughes was
now holding back when it came to tackling for the ball. Ball took the
young midfielder to one side and gave him another rollicking, telling
him that he must never hold back, even if he was playing against the
most famous player in the world.

Emlyn Hughes heeded Alan Ball's words and his fearsome tackling
was to be one of the main reasons for Liverpool boss Bill Shankly being
attracted to him. Alan Ball encouraged Hughes to be no respecter of
reputations when it came to the field of play. Alan Ball himself didn't
think twice about voicing his feelings and he once even gave the

legendary Stanley Matthews a rollicking when he refused to run after a Ball pass because the Blackpool youngster had not played the ball into the maestro's feet where he preferred it.

Fred Hughes continued to keep a close eye on his son's football education at Blackpool and would quiz Emlyn constantly to make sure he was looking after himself. When he travelled back to Barrow after a game on the Saturday, Emlyn Hughes would have to tell his father what he had been up to that week. He was constantly warned not to smoke and drink and to avoid late nights at all costs. Emlyn would still help out in the summer months with the tarmac business, hoping that the coming season would be the one in which he would make a first-team breakthrough.

Another young player at Blackpool at the time was future chief executive of the Football Association Graham Kelly. Kelly's daytime occupation was as an employee of Barclays Bank, and he played several games for the Blackpool 'A' team as a goalkeeper during the mid-1960s. Graham Kelly recalled Emlyn Hughes approaching him after one poor goalkeeping performance and telling him that he was wasting his time at Blackpool: 'I remember Emlyn telling me I'd always be a banker, or something that sounded very similar, after one heavy defeat,' Kelly remarked in his autobiography. 'He, of course, went on to play for England; I did not.' Hughes was clearly never afraid to voice his opinions, even during his early teenage years at Blackpool.

Emlyn Hughes' path to the Blackpool first team came about by chance. He turned up for a Blackpool 'A' team game and was told that the regular left-back was unable to play. Hughes played at full-back for the first time in his life and looked impressive. Emlyn had only been expected to be a reserve for the game, but a twist of fate had thrown him in at the deep end and he had performed well.

He was then selected at left-back for the next six games and looked like he had been playing there all his life. Eric Hayward told Hughes that at long last he looked like he had found his true position. The Blackpool reserve-team left-back John Prentis then found himself out of the game for a long period with a broken leg and in April 1965 Emlyn Hughes made his Central League debut against Blackburn Rovers. They drew 1-1 and a few days later Hughes was selected again for the reserves against Burnley. Once again the game ended in a 1-1 draw.

Emlyn Hughes played throughout the 1965/66 season as an established Central League player, but he was now desperate for a first-team chance. Fred Hughes decided that Emlyn's chances of making the first team needed a helping hand and he took to writing to the Blackpool Saturday-night football newspaper letters page using different *noms de plume*. He would make comments such as, 'When is this young lad Emlyn Hughes going to be given a first team chance?' and 'Emlyn Hughes looks one hell of a prospect. Surely he deserves a chance in the Blackpool team' – all of which had Blackpool supporters asking just who was this exciting young player in their reserve side? Fred Hughes also took to standing near the directors' box shouting, 'Hells bells, this lad at full-back looks useful. He's getting better every game!'

Whether Fred Hughes' one-man campaign to get his son a chance in the first team worked one will never know, but at the end of the 1965/66 season Emlyn Hughes' dream came true. With Blackpool's England players Jimmy Armfield and Alan Ball called up for early training ahead of England's 1966 World Cup campaign, Emlyn Hughes was selected for an end-of-season game at Blackburn Rovers. Regular Blackpool left-back Tommy Thompson was switched to the right to take Armfield's place and Emlyn Hughes came in on the left. The date was 2 May 1966.

Among the spectators at Ewood Park that night was the boss of Liverpool Football Club. His team had just won the First Division title at a canter but, as always, he was relentless in his pursuit of new talent to make his outstanding Liverpool side even more formidable. Recalling the game in his autobiography, Bill Shankly said he couldn't believe his eyes when the action started. Shankly recalled: 'I said to Ronnie Suart, the Blackpool manager, "Who's playing?" and he said, "There is a boy here from Barrow in his first game." He didn't half play! He did everything – even to the extent of getting a player sent off. The player retaliated against Emlyn, who was in the right, and I thought that will upset him, but it didn't. He kept on playing and was cutting inside, and cutting the ball back out. I offered £25,000 for him right after the match. I said to myself, "This is somebody special."'

Shankly also revealed that he had also been alerted to Emlyn Hughes' potential by a mystery letter writer from The Fylde. Whether this was

Fred Hughes up to his old tricks is something we will never know, but Emlyn Hughes' name on the team sheet against Blackburn on that May evening in 1966 was definitely not the first time that the kid from Barrow had been brought to the great man's attention.

Emlyn Hughes thoroughly enjoyed himself on his debut. Fred Hughes had always instilled in him the importance of making his mark early on in a game. When the young full-back kicked the Blackburn hero Bryan Douglas in the first few minutes of play and sent the England winger sprawling over the touchline, he certainly had the crowd up in arms. Emlyn Hughes was waging a one man war against Blackburn and he was enjoying every minute of the experience. Bryan Douglas was an outstanding winger and could easily have given the inexperienced Hughes the runaround. The Blackpool debutant decided to try and nullify Douglas early on and by all accounts achieved his objective.

It is highly likely that Bill Shankly had had one of his backroom staff at Anfield dispatched to Bloomfield Road to check out the young Blackpool full-back in one of his reserve-team appearances. When he found out that Emlyn Hughes was due to make his debut against one of England's finest wingers, it was an opportunity that was too good to miss. No doubt Shankly was tipped off by the mystery letter writer from the Fylde that the subject of his glowing references was due to make his first-team bow.

Also in the crowd that night at Ewood Park was Manchester United boss Sir Matt Busby. It is not recorded whether United's legendary manager was also impressed by Emlyn Hughes' sensational debut, but the following morning's sports pages gave the Blackpool debutant several mentions.

Fred Hughes had advised his son to make a mark for himself as quickly as possible. Apart from laying out Bryan Douglas in the first few minutes, Hughes also became involved in a flare-up with George Jones which resulted in Jones being sent off. He then argued his corner with seasoned Blackburn professionals such as Mike Ferguson and Barry Hole, who were desperately attempting to wind the Blackpool teenager up in an attempt to get him sent off. Hughes just laughed as the Blackburn supporters booed and jeered every time he touched the ball.

A star in the making. Emlyn Hughes pictured just after he broke into the Blackpool first team in 1966. Within months of this photograph being taken Bill Shankly had whisked the talented teenager off to Anfield.

When Blackpool went in 2–0 at half-time, a smiling Ron Suart congratulated Hughes, telling him that he was certainly making a name for himself. Blackpool won the game at a canter and were safe from the threat of relegation for another season. Blackburn Rovers were already relegated, but to be trounced by their Lancashire rivals was the final straw in a dreadful season at Ewood Park.

Although Bill Shankly wanted to take Emlyn Hughes back to Anfield there and then, Blackpool were not in any desperate need for an injection of cash, mainly because their star man Alan Ball was certain to be moving from Bloomfield Road after that summer's World Cup finals had come to an end. After Ball's fantastic displays for England in the 1966 tournament, Blackpool sold him to Everton for the then British record transfer fee of £110,000. For the time being the finances at Bloomfield Road were in a healthy state. Bill Shankly would have loved to have taken Alan Ball to Anfield, but after missing out on one major Blackpool talent, he was determined that he was not going to miss out on the Lancashire club's other young gem. He was determined that Emlyn Hughes would be a Liverpool player before too long.

CHAPTER 4

'I knew he was a winner. There are some players you go to watch and you really think they can play, but you are not too sure. I knew with Emlyn Hughes there was no risk' – Bill Shankly

At the start of the 1966/67 season English football was on a terrific high. Alf Ramsey's 'wingless wonders' had just become World Champions after a glorious summer of football. On Merseyside, Liverpool were League Champions and Everton FA Cup winners. Even at Bloomfield Road, Blackpool were optimistic that the sale of England hero Alan Ball to Everton for £110,000 would allow Ron Suart to delve into the transfer market and build a team capable of relinquishing their tag as one that always seemed to be fighting against relegation.

To Jimmy Armfield and his Blackpool teammates however, the sale of Alan Ball was a kick in the teeth. After impressing against Blackburn at the end of the previous campaign and then looking outstanding in pre-season friendlies, Emlyn Hughes thought he might have been in the side for the start of the new season, but Hughes was not selected for the opening game away to Sheffield Wednesday. As it happened Blackpool lost 3-0 and looked a dejected bunch of players as they trudged back to their dressing room after the match. Jimmy Armfield revealed in his autobiography that it was one of the few occasions when he lost his rag with affable Blackpool boss Ron Suart. Armfield recalled: 'Nothing summed up the state of Blackpool FC better than Ball's departure to Everton in the summer of 1966. They allowed him to leave just weeks after he had played a leading role in England's World Cup victory. He was a national hero and a cult figure in Blackpool, but the club regarded him as expendable and he was sold just before the start of the new season. We had lost our World Cup star and were beaten 3-0.'

Armfield had words with Suart after the game: '"I don't know what was up with you lot out there today," said Ronnie as we sat in the dressing room. "You don't know what was up with us?" I asked. "You go and sell our World Cup winner and then you wonder what's wrong. What do you expect?"'

Emlyn Hughes' next first-team chance came the following week when he came on as a substitute for Johnny Green in Blackpool's game against Southampton. Hughes then kept his place for a midweek game against Leicester City. He played well in a 3-2 defeat and Ron Suart congratulated him on his display after the game.

After that fixture, Emlyn Hughes retained his place in the Blackpool starting line-up until his transfer to Liverpool. 'That game against Southampton was the turning point of my career,' he remarked. 'I held my place ever since.'

With Emlyn Hughes now regarding himself as a first-teamer at Blackpool, under the guidance of Fred Hughes he considered that the time was now right to approach Ron Suart for a wage increase. He was still on £8 a week at Bloomfield Road. The Blackpool manager listened to Hughes put his case for a wage increase and then offered the youngster a wage offer that amounted to £30 a week depending on appearances and bonus payments. Emlyn Hughes could not believe what he had just been offered and after informing his father, sitting in his car outside Bloomfield Road, the two of them celebrated with a slap-up meal. To Emlyn Hughes the high life had arrived.

Bill Shankly continued to track the young Blackpool defender and travelled to watch him in action against Chelsea. Once again, Shankly was to witness a controversial game in which Emlyn Hughes was the main protagonist. It was a League Cup tie at Bloomfield Road and Tommy Docherty's young Chelsea side were one of the top teams in the First Division. They were packed with talent, none more so than the brilliant Peter Osgood, who sadly passed away in 2006. Right from the outset of his Blackpool first-team career, Emlyn Hughes had shown that he was no great respecter of reputations and he got stuck into Osgood from the kick-off. After one brief skirmish, the two players clashed again in a no-holds-barred tackle. Unfortunately, Osgood came out of the tackle with a broken leg and had to be carried off on a stretcher. The rest of the Chelsea team then had it in for Hughes for the remainder of the game, which ended in a draw. Bill Shankly spoke to Emlyn Hughes after the match and confirmed to the concerned Blackpool youngster that it was a 50/50 ball that was there to be won and that he had done nothing wrong.

Although Bill Shankly's words put Emlyn Hughes' mind at ease, when he walked out at Stamford Bridge for the replay a week later he knew that he would be up against it. An hour before kick-off, Tommy Docherty even issued a warning to Hughes that he had instructed every one of his team to try and break his leg in the game. Emlyn informed the Blackpool manager of Docherty's threat, but the Chelsea boss vehemently denied the player's allegation. As it turned out, Emlyn Hughes came through the game relatively unscathed and Blackpool put in a great performance to win the replay 3-1. In later years, Hughes remarked that there was never any lingering bad feeling between himself and Chelsea and that he always got on well with Docherty and Osgood when their paths crossed.

In the first game at Bloomfield Road, Bill Shankly had once again seen Emlyn Hughes come through a full-blooded encounter against First Division opposition with flying colours. Although he was on the books of another club, Shankly now regarded Hughes as a Liverpool player. He even took to ringing him up on Sunday mornings to check what he was about to eat for his breakfast. Emlyn Hughes recounted the story years later of his Sunday morning phone calls from the Liverpool manager: 'I'd be just about to make short work of a plate of eggs, bacon and black pudding, when the phone would ring. It would be Shanks, "Hey, Emlyn son, don't eat that stuff you've got on your plate there. I'll be signing you soon. I want you lean and hungry son. Lean and hungry!" Thirty years later I still associate the smell of bacon frying with the telephone ringing at 8.30 sharp on a Sunday morning.'

Bill Shankly was not the only person beginning to sit up and take notice during the 1966/67 season. Television viewers in the Granada region would see highlights of north-west teams in action in a Sunday afternoon programme. Emlyn Hughes made football fans throughout the region were aware of his all-action style of play in a televised game against Blackpool's Lancashire rivals Manchester City. Although Hughes was still playing as a full-back, he was always looking for the opportunity to burst forward and hit a piledriver of a shot at the opposition goal. Bill Shankly probably dreaded the whole region being made aware of Emlyn Hughes' undoubted football prowess and the day when he had his precious signature on the dotted line of a Liverpool contract could not come soon enough for the Reds boss.

Although Blackpool again struggled in the First Division during Emlyn Hughes' last season at the club, it was a different story in the League Cup. They fought their way through to the quarter-finals, where they met West Ham at Bloomfield Road. On the same evening that Bill Shankly's Liverpool were slaughtered 5-1 in Amsterdam by Johann Cruyff's Ajax, Blackpool took on West Ham for a League Cup semi-final place.

Emlyn Hughes once again lined up at left-back against a star-studded West Ham team. World Cup stars Bobby Moore, Martin Peters and Geoff Hurst were all in the Hammers' team as they trotted out at Bloomfield Road. The fact that only 15,000 turned out for the game illustrates the fact that, while the rest of the country was enjoying a football boom after the World Cup success, Blackpool really were a club struggling to hold on to their First Division status.

Emlyn Hughes and his teammates were only two games away from their first Wembley appearance since 1953, but it was England star Geoff Hurst, who stole all the headlines. Hurst was on fire after his World Cup adventures and he scored the opener after just two minutes. He struck again twenty minutes later to notch his twenty-sixth goal of the season. When one considers that it was still only the beginning of December, it gives you an idea of the rich vein of form that Geoff Hurst was in during that period in his career.

With the West Ham defence being brilliantly marshalled by Bobby Moore, Blackpool were given few chances to fight their way back into the game. West Ham struck again early in the second half through Johnny Byrne to make the game safe. Ray Charnley scored Blackpool's only goal of the game, Bobby Moore's men running out 3-1 winners.

Bill Shankly, the Liverpool boss who tried to sign the teenage Emlyn Hughes
after witnessing his Blackpool debut against Blackburn Rovers in May 1966. The
following year Shankly brought Hughes back to Merseyside in the back of his car.
Hughes described Bill Shankly as second to only his own father, Fred Hughes, as the
greatest man who ever lived.

Emlyn Hughes would have loved the opportunity to have played at Wembley, but he would have to wait until his Liverpool and England days – when the stadium would become almost a second home.

With Emlyn Hughes now a permanent fixture in the Blackpool side, football fans throughout the country were being treated to the impressive full-back displays of the Blackpool youngster on a regular basis. Future Liverpool favourite and European Cup hero Joey Jones revealed in his autobiography that although he was a Reds fanatic, the first big match that he ever attended was at Goodison Park – it was Everton against Blackpool during the 1966/67 season. Joey travelled with his father from their home in Llandudno on a works outing. Joey Jones' dad Harry was certainly impressed by the young lad playing at left-back for Blackpool that day: 'The Hotpoint factory ran a trip once a year to see Liverpool or Everton play. It was Everton against Blackpool this one year and Emlyn Hughes was playing for Blackpool. My dad said to me that day he thought Hughes was the type of player Liverpool should sign. A few weeks later, I ran back with the *Liverpool Echo* to tell him Hughes had signed. He said, "I told you so."'

With the likes of Don Revie at Leeds and other top managers now fully aware of Emlyn Hughes' incredible potential, Bill Shankly knew that he had to act first. Shankly's opportunity came when Blackpool sacked Ron Suart. The man who had given Emlyn Hughes the opportunity to make a career for himself in professional football was replaced by Blackpool legend Stan Mortenson, the former Bloomfield Road hero whose hat-trick had won the club the FA Cup in 1953.

Suart contacted Hughes to ask him to visit him at his home to discuss the young full-back's future. Ron Suart told Emlyn Hughes that when the youngster arrived at Blackpool he was not impressed at all. He had only given him a chance because he was from the same home town of Barrow-in-Furness as himself, and also to do a favour for Emlyn's father. Suart's opinion of Hughes' footballing ability had now, however, changed beyond all recognition. Hughes was informed that virtually every club in the First Division wanted him, but Suart had decided that Liverpool would be his choice. No doubt the mystery letter writer from The Fylde also had some input into Roy Suart's preferred choice of club for Emlyn Hughes! For some time now the

Blackpool teenager had been guided in the direction of Liverpool and Bill Shankly and to Emlyn Hughes and his dad Fred it was a marriage made in heaven. Liverpool were the reigning League Champions and, crucially for Fred Hughes, within travelling distance of Barrow. Fred had kept a close eye on every stage of his son's blossoming career in football and he was not about to stop now.

CHAPTER 5

'Shanks took me to one side and said go out there and give them some-thing to remember' – Emlyn Hughes on his infamous rugby tackle on Newcastle's Albert Bennett that led to him being nicknamed 'Crazy Horse'.

It was not until Blackpool made the decision to show Ron Suart the door that Emlyn Hughes considered leaving the club. Bill Shankly had made no secret of his desire to take him to Anfield, but during the 1960s this was not regarded as 'tapping up' a player. Shankly had contact with numerous players and managers, even the ones he missed out on such as Alan Ball. He would often phone them up to talk football. Nowadays this would obviously be frowned upon, but in the 1960s football fanatics like Shankly could keep up a regular contact with whichever player they wanted to. Bill Shankly was probably one of the few who actually carried out this activity with players, but it was not regarded as a big deal.

With Blackpool looking certainties to be relegated at the end of the season, the club felt it was probably now time to cash in on Emlyn Hughes. Ron Suart had told Hughes to sit tight at Blackpool and to wait for Liverpool to sort out the transfer. Suart then con-tacted Shankly and the transfer of Emlyn Hughes to Anfield was set in motion. A fee of £65,000 was agreed and Hughes played his last game for Blackpool on 25 February 1967 against Manchester United. He had made 26 League and 6 cup appearances for the Lancashire club. On 27 February he joined Liverpool. After fighting against relegation for several seasons, Blackpool lost their First Division status at the end of the 1966/67 campaign. For Emlyn Hughes, however, the next stage in his sensational career had only just begun.

When Bill Shankly turned up at Blackpool to tie up Hughes' transfer, he brought along a Liverpool director, Sidney Reakes. Emlyn Hughes was accompanied by his older brother David and his father Fred. Hughes was surprised when Reakes complied with Shankly's request for him to leave the room while the Liverpool boss talked money. Emlyn Hughes had a request of his own, which was to wait until his brother and father arrived before finances were discussed. Shankly agreed to this and at the end of negotiations Hughes was informed that his earnings potential at Anfield would be in the region of £120 per week depending on bonuses and appearance money.

Emlyn Hughes and his family were delighted with the outcome and thought they would now have a few days to sort things out. The idiosyncratic Liverpool boss however informed them that he would be driving his new star capture back to Merseyside there and then. Hughes was surprised, but after picking up his belongings from his digs at Levens Grove, and bidding farewell to his landlady Mrs Mawson he was on his way to Liverpool.

Emlyn Hughes' journey back to Merseyside with Bill Shankly has been recounted many times, but for the record this is what happened. After travelling for a few miles, Bill Shankly, who might have been a brilliant football manager but was not noted for his driving skills, was involved in an incident with another vehicle. After first attempting to overtake another car, he then changed his mind and a car drove into the back of him, smashing his rear lights. Straight away, Shankly was out of the car and on the attack. When the dust settled, numbers were exchanged and the Liverpool boss continued on his journey to Merseyside. A police motorcyclist then pulled Shankly over for having damaged rear lights. What happened next astounded Emlyn Hughes. After explaining to the policeman about the accident and telling him that as soon as he got back to Liverpool he would have the car repaired, the policeman explained to Shankly that he shouldn't be on the road with no rear lights working. 'You stupid man,' roared the Liverpool manager. 'How am I supposed to get home? Don't you know who's sitting in this car with me?' The bemused policeman scratched his head and said he had no idea either who he was, or the car's other occupant. 'There sits the future captain of England!' Shankly exclaimed before getting into the car and driving off. Emlyn Hughes at this stage in his two-hour-old Liverpool career must have thought he was being driven back to Merseyside by a madman. As it was to turn out, Bill Shankly was destined to become almost like a second father to him before too long.

Emlyn Hughes must have been taken aback by Bill Shankly's bold claim that he would one day be captain of England. This was one Shankly prediction that was destined to come true. It is interesting to note, however, that Shankly was not averse to making astounding predictions about players who had only played a handful of League games right from the outset of his managerial career. Some years earlier when he was manager at Workington, he made similar predictions about his goalkeeper Wilf Billington, after a hard-fought game against Tranmere Rovers at Prenton Park. Shankly told the few members of the press present that Billington would be the England goalkeeper within two years. The men from the press looked puzzled as they scribbled the name of Billington into their notebooks. Wilf went on to play 52 games for Workington before disappearing from League football. To Bill Shankly, however, at that moment in time Wilf Billington was a certain star of the future. With a manager who had such faith and confidence in his players it is small wonder that his teams played out of their skins for him.

No doubt Bill Shankly talked Emlyn Hughes' head off about football on the drive back to Liverpool. Hughes recalled that Shankly mentioned he quite liked the colour of traffic lights – red, just like Liverpool! The Everton jokes must have also come thick and fast. A particular Shankly favourite was the one about the Everton manager not being in good health – he's got a bad side! By the time Bill Shankly dropped him off at his temporary accommodation at Liverpool's Lord Nelson Hotel, Emlyn Hughes knew everything there was to know about Liverpool Football Club and why they and their supporters were the greatest in the world.

To Bill Shankly, capturing Hughes was a fantastic piece of business. In his autobiography the Liverpool boss described it as 'one of the major signings of all time'. He often joked that he was afraid to go back to Blackpool after signing Hughes in case they locked him up for daylight robbery! The £65,000 fee that Liverpool paid for the teenager was, at the time, quite a substantial sum for a teenager who had yet to complete a full season of First Division football. As it was to turn out, it was one of the greatest bits of transfer activity that Liverpool Football Club were ever involved in.

At the time it was quite unusual for Bill Shankly to sign a player from a fellow First Division Club. The likes of Gordon Milne, Ron Yeats, Ian St John, Willie Stevenson, Peter Thompson and, in later years, Alec Lindsay, Larry Lloyd, Ray Clemence and Kevin Keegan all came from outside the First Division. The rest of the Liverpool side was made up from home-grown talent such as Chris Lawler, Tommy Smith, Gerry Bryne, Roger Hunt, Bobby Graham, Tommy Lawrence, Brian Hall and Steve Heighway. Shankly was certain that Emlyn Hughes would be a success at Anfield. 'I knew he was a winner. I knew there was no risk,' said the Liverpool boss about the kid from Barrow.

Emlyn Hughes made his Liverpool debut at Anfield against Stoke City on 4 March 1967. Goals from Lawler and Hunt gave the Reds a 2-1 victory. Hughes played at left-back in place of the injured Gerry Bryne. Hughes made a sound debut and although he was still a little raw, most Liverpool fans had seen the teenager playing for Blackpool on television and knew what an outstanding prospect he was.

A week later, one of the biggest derby matches of the post-war years was due to take place at Goodison Park. It was the fifth round of the FA Cup and the clamour for tickets was so great that eight giant screens were erected at Anfield to enable the game to be viewed on a closed-circuit transmission. At Goodison and Anfield over 105,000 fans gathered to see Alan Ball win the game for Everton with the only goal of the game. Emlyn Hughes had to sit out this game due to being cup-tied after an appearance for Blackpool in that year's FA Cup. As he sat at Goodison witnessing the incredible passion of a pulsating Merseyside derby, he must have been made patently aware of just what a hotbed of football he would now be plying his trade in.

Emlyn Hughes returned to the Liverpool side for an away game a week later at Burnley. Liverpool lost 1-0 and were beginning to lose ground on the side that would emerge as League Champions at the end of the 1966/67 season, Manchester United. United were

Liverpool's next opponents at Anfield and came away with a point after a 0-0 draw. At this stage Emlyn Hughes was already a regular in the Liverpool side, Bill Shankly still playing him at left back. Shankly was satisfied with Hughes' displays, knowing that it would take him a little time to bed in at Anfield.

For Liverpool as a club, however, the 1966/67 season had been a major disappointment. Ajax had slaughtered them in the European Cup and an Alan Ball-inspired Everton had ended their FA Cup dreams. George Best and his Old Trafford teammates were romping ahead in the race for the League title.

Bill Shankly told Emlyn Hughes that the Anfield faithful needed something to cheer them up after what had been, by Liverpool's standards, a miserable season. Liverpool were due to play Newcastle United at Anfield on 7 April 1967. 'Go out there son and give them something to remember; they need a new hero' were Bill Shankly's words of advice before Liverpool took on Newcastle. Shankly had witnessed at first hand Hughes' dynamic debut for Blackpool against Blackburn the previous season, the Liverpool fans hadn't. He wanted them to feel what he felt when he witnessed the strapping teenager waging a one-man war against a First Division side. Emlyn Hughes had had a few games to get used to life at Anfield. Shankly now wanted to see him unleash hell against the opposition in the red shirt of Liverpool in the same way that he once had in the tangerine of Blackpool.

Emlyn Hughes ran out against Newcastle determined to carry out his manager's orders, but just what he would do even he probably didn't know. Shankly had told him to make an impression. Emlyn's dad Fred had also often told his son to do something to get noticed in a game. After half an hour against Newcastle, Emlyn Hughes' chance came. Hughes had been receiving a bit of a runaround by Newcastle's flying right-winger, Albert Bennett. Using his speed off the mark to great advantage, Bennett skipped past the young full-back time and time again and was beginning to make a monkey out of Liverpool's new signing. Bennett flicked the ball past Hughes again and was just about to sprint past him to set up a goalscoring chance for Newcastle. Unbelievably, Emlyn Hughes decided that the only way to stop Bennett was to rugby tackle him neck-high to bring the startled winger to the ground. The watching Fred Hughes must have thought he was back at Craven Park watching his beloved Barrow Rugby League Club, not Anfield for a game of football. Emlyn Hughes had been told to give the crowd something to remember, but Bill Shankly hadn't quite had this in mind. Shankly, Paisley, Fagan and the rest of the Liverpool bench began to laugh when they recovered from the shock.

The whole of Anfield thought it was hilarious as they waited to see if their team would now have to play Newcastle with a man short. As Albert Bennett got to his feet rubbing his neck, Emlyn Hughes waited for the referee to administer his punishment. The referee, fortunately for Hughes, was also laughing his head off. When he regained his composure, he gave Hughes a ticking-off, but didn't even bother taking his name. Football fans in 2006 might find it unbelievable, but Emlyn Hughes got off scot-free. Football was definitely a funnier game in the 1960s. Shankly had told Emlyn Hughes to give the crowd something to remember and he had delivered.

The incident was seen that evening on *Match of the Day* and the whole country thought it was highly amusing. It was seen as more daft than vicious and the legend of 'Crazy Horse' was born. Emlyn Hughes in his autobiography claimed that the Albert Bennett incident was the start of the 'Crazy Horse' nickname.

There is however an alternative theory on the origins of the nickname. Among the millions watching Emlyn's antics against Albert Bennett were a great many Evertonians and, according to some, it was the blue half of Merseyside and not the red who christened Hughes 'Crazy Horse'. It has to be remembered that Merseyside homes are often split, with some of the family Evertonians and the rest Liverpool supporters. The theory goes that what was started as a term of abuse by Everton fans, was taken up by Liverpudlians as a tribute to their new hero.

Emlyn Hughes himself said that he didn't particularly like the 'Crazy Horse' nickname at first, but he grew to like it as time went by – similar in many ways to Bill 'Dixie' Dean with his dislike of his famous nickname.

Whatever the origins, 'Crazy Horse' seemed to be apt for a young player who appeared to have boundless energy and a galloping running style with his arms flailing away as he switched from defence to attack throughout the whole ninety minutes' play. As he showed against the

An early shot of Emlyn Hughes during his first season at Anfield. His new teammates were bowled over by Hughes' tremendous energy and all-action style. He never stopped running for the whole ninety minutes. He had built up his stamina by running along the beach at Walney Island for hours on end during his teenage years back home in Barrow.

hapless Albert Bennett, Hughes was certainly an unpredictable young player during his early days at Anfield, similar in many ways to a young horse that hadn't been broken in yet.

One thing that Emlyn Hughes' rugby tackle on Albert Bennett did achieve was to make Hughes an instant hit with the Kop. Liverpool won the game against Newcastle 3-1 through two goals, one from Roger Hunt and the other from Ian Callaghan. The biggest cheer of the day, however, went to Emlyn Hughes. A new Liverpool hero was born and the canny Bill Shankly had been proved correct yet again. It should be noted however that Fred Hughes, who was at the game with Emlyn's mother Anne, had also given his son exactly the same advice before the match about doing something to get noticed.

CHAPTER 6

'If they don't accept you fair and square I'll get rid of the lot of them'
– Bill Shankly to Emlyn Hughes after he was initially rejected
by some of his teammates at Liverpool.

Emlyn Hughes might have been an instant hit with the Liverpool
faithful after just a handful of games for the Reds, but with his new
teammates it was an uneasy start at Anfield. Anyone who has ever had
the pleasure of being in the company of the Liverpool players of the
1960s cannot have failed to have noticed certain characteristics about
them. To this day they remain a very close-knit group of men. They are
down to earth and modest and any football fan, no matter which team
they support, would feel comfortable talking football with them.

This is the small squad of players who set in motion Bill Shankly's
dream of Liverpool becoming one of the greatest club teams in
the world. Five European Cups later, Liverpool Football Club have
fulfilled most of Shankly's early aspirations and it was the likes of Yeats,
St John, and all the other 1960s heroes who set Liverpool's climb to
global fame in motion.

By the time Emlyn Hughes joined Liverpool in 1967, Shankly's
team had won two First Division titles and the FA Cup. They had also
come incredibly close to reaching the European Cup final in 1965,
only to be denied this by a talented Inter Milan side and some dodgy
refereeing decisions in the semi-final. Most of the side had experienced
international football. In a nutshell they had done it all.

When Emlyn Hughes joined Liverpool he hadn't even played a full
season in the First Division. Despite this, he was extremely confident in
his own ability. This is what Bill Shankly liked about him. This is why

he had no qualms about paying what was at the time a large amount of money for a teenager. Emlyn had been brought up by his dad to be a confident player and to have no fears about voicing his opinions on football or whatever else was under discussion. Some of the established players at Liverpool viewed Emlyn's confident attitude to football and life in general as cockiness and they didn't like it. Ian St John stated in his recent autobiography that Emlyn Hughes had two personas, one that the players saw and one that the public saw.

Liverpool Echo journalist Ian Hargreaves interviewed Emlyn Hughes on a regular basis during the player's Liverpool career and concluded in his book *Liverpool Greats*, 'I have always found him a pleasant and considerate person whose worst fault appeared to be the usually laudable quality of over enthusiasm.' There is little doubt that Emlyn Hughes found it hard to be accepted by his teammates at Liverpool when he joined the club in 1967. He said in his autobiography, 'I was a bit like an outsider trying to force his way into a private members club. We seemed to be on different wavelengths at times.'

Bill Shankly took his squad's lukewarm reception to his new signing from Blackpool badly. Shankly had always preached that Liverpool Football Club and their supporters came first, not who the team liked and disliked. He made no secret of the fact that he didn't give a damn whether his players liked or disliked him as long as they performed with distinction for Liverpool on the field of play. As it was, though, most of Shankly's players thought the world of him. Bill Shankly took his team's cold treatment of Emlyn Hughes personally and told him that there would be a mass clear-out of his entire Liverpool squad before he would allow the young defender to be forced out.

Emlyn Hughes played out the final games of the 1966/67 season in an unhappy frame of mind. Liverpool lost 3 of their final 5 games, including a 3-1 home defeat at Anfield to Hughes' former club Blackpool, who had already been relegated. A George Best-inspired Manchester United won the title by four points from Nottingham Forest, Liverpool finishing a disappointing fifth.

Apart from feeling rejected by some members of the Liverpool squad, Emlyn Hughes also disliked living in a city centre hotel. Living in digs in Blackpool he had been well looked after by a caring landlady,

Emlyn Hughes in action for Liverpool against Chelsea in January 1969.

but returning to a hotel where he knew no one was driving him up the wall.

Together with another Liverpool youngster, Peter Wall, he moved into digs where he would be well looked after with plenty of good home cooking. The house was in Lawrence Road, Wavertree and the landlady, Minnie Firth, was the mother of a friend of the two Liverpool players, Ken Firth. Another star Shankly signing, Alan Evans, from Wolves, was also destined to end up lodging in the Firth household.

Along with Peter Wall, Emlyn Hughes would sometimes spend an evening at the local dog track near Wavertree known as the White City. Hughes had always been fond of a flutter since he was a youngster back in Barrow. Eventually, life at Liverpool was destined to become happier. Fred and Anne Hughes visited the city regularly to keep their son's spirits up.

Hughes' new teammates might have been distinctly unimpressed with what they perceived as the somewhat self-centred nature the young defender possessed. When it came to his footballing ability, however, to a man they were beginning to be bowled over. Emlyn Hughes might not have been the most skilful of players but when it came to fantastic enthusiasm, 'Crazy Horse' was second to none. Emlyn's ability to run from box to box for the whole ninety minutes also delighted Bill Shankly and the Liverpool coaching staff. They knew that Hughes' incredible stamina needed to be utilised more fully. Quite frankly, he was wasted at full-back. Bill Shankly had himself been known as the 'Human Dynamo' during his playing days at Preston North End because of his non-stop running. Shankly's chief lieutenant at Anfield, Bob Paisley, had also been an all-action midfielder during his playing days for Liverpool. Along with the rest of the Anfield coaching staff they could plainly see that Emlyn Hughes was in the same mould as themselves. When training began for the 1967/68 season at Liverpool, Hughes was earmarked to replace Anfield favourite Willie Stevenson at left-half in the team. It was in this position that Emlyn Hughes' career at Liverpool would begin to blossom.

CHAPTER 7

'Emlyn had a great personality and he was always up for a laugh. Nothing daunted him, even as a raw youngster at Liverpool' – Roger Hunt

Emlyn Hughes began the 1967/68 season at Liverpool with the no.6 shirt on his back. He was destined to wear that shirt for the next eleven years at Anfield, although by the time he left for Wolves in 1979, his days as a marauding midfielder had long been over.

It was while touring Germany before the start of the new campaign that Bill Shankly decided to blood Hughes as a midfielder. Liverpool were on a pre-season tour of Germany and Hughes was asked by Shankly to do a man-marking job on Cologne's outstanding German international, Wolfgang Overath. Apart from keeping tabs on Overath, Hughes was also told to join in Liverpool's attacking play when they had the ball.

Emlyn Hughes looked outstanding in his new role, not giving Overath a kick of the ball and then roving about the pitch to join in the Reds' forward moves. Overath became frustrated by the total domination that the young Liverpool player had over him and decided to try and kick Hughes out of the game. Not afraid to look after himself when the occasion demanded, Hughes decided to give Overath a little reminder that he cared little for his reputation as one of Germany's finest. Noticing that the referee looked like he might give Emlyn Hughes his marching orders, Bob Paisley then shouted for him to lie down and pretend to be injured. Paisley's ploy worked and Emlyn was carried off on a stretcher, although he didn't have the slightest injury and substitute Geoff Strong replaced him. Bill Shankly didn't want to have a player sent off in a friendly and risk Hughes receiving a suspension before the domestic campaign had even begun. Emlyn Hughes, however, had shown enough in his performance at wing-half for Bill Shankly to select him at left-half for the beginning of the new season.

Liverpool also had a new striker for the coming season. Tony Hateley was signed by Shankly from Chelsea for a £96,000 fee. After the disappointments of the previous campaign, Bill Shankly knew his side needed revitalising and in just his second game for the Reds, Hately knocked in a hat-trick in an emphatic 6-0 victory over Nottingham Forest. Anfield legend Roger Hunt, scored two of the other goals and Anfield heralded a new 'H-Bombers' strike force. The fact that Emlyn Hughes scored Liverpool's other goal in the victory, the first goal of his First Division career, was the icing on the cake. Bill Shankly just might have found a combination that would take his team back to the forefront of English football sooner than he thought.

Emlyn Hughes also had his first taste of European football at the beginning of the 1967/68 campaign. Liverpool took on Malmö in the European Fairs Cup and a Tony Hateley double gave them a 2-0 victory in the first leg played on 19 September 1967. At this stage of the season, Emlyn Hughes had bedded into the side in the left-half slot vacated by Willie Stevenson who was destined to move on to Stoke City before the year was out.

Liverpool suffered just four defeats in the months leading up to the new year and in Europe they had also moved smoothly into the third round of the Fairs Cup. Their most impressive display of the season so far came in Europe when they slaughtered top German side TSV Munich 8-0 at Anfield. Liverpool were sensational that night against the Germans and Bill Shankly was confident that his first success in Europe as a manager was on the cards. Shankly's dreams were shattered in the very next round when Hungarian side Ferencvaros knocked Liverpool out 2-0 on aggregate in two games played on snow-covered pitches. Perhaps the Hungarians were more familiar with the conditions. Whatever the reasons were, Liverpool had once again been found wanting in Europe.

To Emlyn Hughes, however, travelling abroad and tasting European competition was a dream come true. It was all a far cry from life at

Blackpool and he was now beginning to enjoy life at Anfield more. Some of his antics on away trips still rubbed his teammates up the wrong way, like his habit of grabbing the first meal the waiter put onto the table whether he had ordered it or not. It might have been fish when he had asked for steak, but Emlyn would see no harm in claiming it as his own and would begin to scoff it without a care in the world. The young Emlyn Hughes was more playful than malicious and probably saw no harm in carrying out such a prank. To some of his teammates, however, Emlyn was out of order and although they recognised that he was destined to become a great player, they still found some of his antics tiresome.

On the field of play Emlyn Hughes' confidence as a midfielder was growing with every game. Liverpool were looking a good bet to end the season as League Champions and in the FA Cup they had reached the quarter-finals. Their FA Cup dream, however, came to an end when West Bromwich Albion knocked them out 2-1 after three hard-fought encounters, with the third game taking place at Maine Road. After knocking out Liverpool, West Brom went on to break the hearts of another Merseyside team when a Jeff Astle goal beat Everton in the final.

In the First Division hopes were high that Bill Shankly would win his third title as manager, but Joe Mercer's Manchester City pipped them by three points. Liverpool finished third, with Manchester United the runners-up.

It had been an eventful first full season at Anfield for Emlyn Hughes and in the following year he was destined to win his much coveted first full cap for England.

CHAPTER 8

'I don't know where Emlyn got his energy from, but if you could have packaged him, it would have done the whole nation a lot of good because he never stopped' – Ian St John

Bill Shankly was obviously very disappointed to have missed out on the League title by such a narrow margin in the previous campaign and decided to give his squad an extra boost for the new season.

Shankly was gradually moving out some of the 1966 title-winning team and introducing what he regarded as the best young players in the country to his squad. His decision to spend £65,000 on Emlyn Hughes had paid off handsomely, but the £100,000 he forked out for Wolves teenager Alun Evans was more of a gamble. Evans had impressed Shankly when he had given Ron Yeats a hard time in the colours of Wolves and when he became available the Scot decided to bring him to Anfield.

Once again Liverpool went close in the League, finishing as runners-up to Don Revie's Leeds United with Everton's up-and-coming young side finishing third. In the FA Cup, Leicester City knocked them out of the competition and in the 1968/69 European Fairs Cup Liverpool bowed out to Spanish side Athletic Bibao. Bilbao won the first leg 2-1 and Liverpool won the second leg by the same score, with Emlyn Hughes scoring his first goal in a European competition. After extra time the game was decided on the toss of a coin and Shankly's men were somewhat cruelly dumped out of the competition in the first round.

Emlyn Hughes had personal cause for celebration at the start of the 1969/70 campaign when he was awarded his first England cap by Alf Ramsey. The game took place on 5 November 1969. The opposition was Holland and a Colin Bell goal gave England a 1-0 victory. Although Hughes was now employed by Liverpool at left-half, Ramsey selected him at left-back. Emlyn Hughes made a solid start to his England career and he was to win 62 caps before his international career came to an end in 1980.

The barren spell for Liverpool in terms of silverware continued during the 1969/70 season. They finished in fifth spot in the League, 15 points behind Champions Everton. In the FA Cup, Watford knocked them out 1-0 and it was after this cup defeat that Bill Shankly really started to break up the nucleus of the 1966 title-winning side, the majority of whom were still representing Liverpool. Ron Yeats, Roger Hunt, Ian St John, Tommy Lawrence and other 1960s legends were gradually sold off. They were replaced by the likes of Ray Clemence, Larry Lloyd, Alec Lindsay, Steve Heighway, Brian Hall and one of Shankly's greatest ever signings, Kevin Keegan. If Emlyn Hughes possessed endless stamina and incredible enthusiasm, Keegan also had these two attributes in equal measures.

The only bright spot for Emlyn Hughes at the end of the 1969/70 season was the fact that Alf Ramsey had selected him for the England squad for the 1970 World Cup finals in Mexico. It looked like Ramsey would stick with Leeds defender Terry Cooper in the left-back spot in the team, but Hughes was still proud to be part of the squad.

Emlyn Hughes also had his first taste of the television studios as an entertainer when he sang on the number one hit single 'Back Home'. The squad, dressed in evening suits, made three appearances on *Top of the Pops* and knocked Norman Greenbaum's 'Spirit in the Sky' from the top of the charts. The record was in the charts for sixteen weeks.

Alf Ramsey organised a number of warm-up games for England in South America to help them acclimatise to the high altitude they would have to play at when the tournament began. Emlyn Hughes was selected for the final friendly in what was an England 'B' team. They took on the Ecuadorian champions Liga and Jeff Astle scored a hat-trick with Emlyn Hughes scoring England's other goal in a 4-1 win.

Fred and Anne Hughes flew out to Mexico for the tournament in the hope that their son would get selected by Ramsey for at least one

The man who made Emlyn Hughes' dream of playing for England come true,
Sir Alf Ramsey. Hughes was a mainstay of Ramsey's team from 1970 until the man
who led England to World Cup glory in 1966 lost the management position in 1974.

Members of the England squad, Jeff Astle, Emlyn Hughes and Geoff Hurst listen to a copy of 'Back Home' before flying out from Heathrow Airport for the 1970 World Cup finals in Mexico. 'Back Home' was number one in the pop charts for three weeks.

of the group matches. Fred was interviewed by the *Liverpool Echo* and told them that he was out in Mexico to see his 'soccer son' as opposed to his 'rugby son' David, who at the time was playing for Barrow. Fred said that he was proud of Emlyn, but was not a particularly big fan of the round ball game. 'If there was a rugby match here tomorrow and Brazil were also playing in another stadium, I know which one I'd watch,' declared Fred. 'There's too much play-acting in football' was Fred Hughes' assessment of Emlyn's chosen profession.

England's exit from the competition at the hands of Germany sent the England team back home in a dejected frame of mind, none more so than Emlyn Hughes who failed to play in a single game. 'It's the only regret I've got in the game, that I didn't play in a World Cup final,' declared Emlyn in later years. He was on the bench for two of the matches but Ramsey never used him.

England new boy Emlyn Hughes in 1970.

Emlyn Hughes was back in the England team for the first match after their disappointing World Cup when he was named in the starting line-up for the match against East Germany in November 1970. He was then virtually an ever-present until Don Revie took over as England boss in 1975.

CHAPTER 9

'The energy that had been a vital part of my game simply deserted me in the 1971 FA Cup final' – Emlyn Hughes

The 1970/71 season would be the one when Emlyn Hughes played in an FA Cup final at Wembley for the first time. Bill Shankly had dispatched with Tony Hateley up front and Roger Hunt had also played his last game for the club. The Liverpool of the 1970s was taking shape and Steve Heighway and John Toshack were destined to become exciting figures in the Reds' attack as the season progressed.

Emlyn Hughes was still employed by Shankly as an attacking mid-fielder and during the final game of the season against Southampton at Anfield in April 1971 he scored what many believed to be his greatest goal for Liverpool. After defending a Southampton move one minute, within seconds he was setting up an attack with a pass to the wing. He then surged forward to the edge of the Southampton penalty area to receive the ball back before hitting a scorching shot past the startled goalkeeper.

The Kop went wild as Emlyn Hughes celebrated as only he could, running around the pitch, his hands flailing away in windmill fashion like a demented version of The Who guitarist Pete Townshend. The broad grin on Hughes' face remained there until the end of the game, which Liverpool won 1-0.

Emlyn Hughes scored eight goals during the 1970/71 League campaign and did not miss a single game through injury. Emlyn Hughes' ability to steer clear of injury until the final season of his career at Liverpool was quite remarkable. The fact that only the quite phenomenal Ian Callaghan, who made 843 appearances for the Reds, played

more games for the club than Hughes tells you something about the
high fitness levels he sustained throughout his Anfield career.

Apart from reaching the FA Cup final, the main highlights of the
1970/71 season for Liverpool were reaching the semi-final of the European
Fairs Cup and the fantastic derby victory over Everton at Anfield. Leeds
knocked Liverpool out of the Fairs Cup 1-0 on aggregate after two tense
encounters in the semi-final. Liverpool's 3-2 victory over Everton at
Anfield in November 1970 had to be seen to be believed. Everton were
the reigning League Champions at the time. Everton dominated the first
half, but found Ray Clemence in brilliant form to deny them. In the
second half, goals from Whittle and Royle put the Blues into what looked
an unassailable lead. Liverpool had the recently signed John Toshack
making only his second appearance for the team and after Heighway gave
the Reds hope, making the score 2-1, the Welsh striker equalised from a
Heighway centre. The Liverpool fans went wild when eight minutes from
the end Chris Lawler hit the winner. After a fabulous derby victory over
Everton, Bill Shankly told the press that it was achieved with the youngest
team that Liverpool had ever selected against the old enemy.

The omens looked good for the future and when Liverpool took on
Everton again in an FA Cup semi-final clash at Old Trafford Shankly
was confident that his young side would triumph again. A full house
turned up at Manchester for the 27 March game for a place in the 1971
FA Cup final. Alan Ball gave Everton the lead, but Steve Heighway was
at his dazzling best and he set up both Alun Evans and Brian Hall to
give the Reds a memorable 2-1 victory. Bill Shankly's up-and-coming
young team had reached their first major final.

The only members of the victorious 1965 FA Cup-winning side
still representing the Reds were Lawler, Smith and Callaghan. Peter
Thompson made an appearance as a substitute for Alun Evans in the
second half. The average age of Shankly's new team was just twenty-
two, but they were beginning to display a solidness and maturity that
belied their tender years.

They were due to face Bertie Mee's Arsenal in the FA Cup final
and the Londoners' side was packed with experienced campaigners
such as Frank McLintock, George Graham, Bob Wilson and George
Armstrong. Arsenal had Steve Heighway marked out as Liverpool's

main danger man and instructed their number one enforcer, Peter Storey, to hit him with some hard tackles as early in the match as possible. The job that Storey did on Heighway reminded older Liverpool fans of the 1950 final when Arsenal's Alex Forbes negated Billy Liddell's impact on the match with some crunching early tackles.

Steve Heighway managed to free himself from the shackles of Storey and beat Bob Wilson for the opening goal of the game in the second half. It looked like Liverpool would give Bill Shankly his first silverware since 1966. Arsenal, however, were bidding to become the first team to complete the League and FA Cup double since Spurs in 1961 and Mee's men were a resilient outfit. The Gunners scored a scrappy equaliser after sixty-three minutes through a Kelly shot that somehow managed to roll across the line from the faintest of Graham touches. Both Emlyn Hughes and Tommy Smith had failed to clear the danger and Smith described Graham's equaliser as 'a bloody stupid goal'. A dejected Emlyn Hughes said after the game, 'I was just too tired to really jump to stop the equalising goal. Then the ball hit Tommy Smith on the chest and before we knew it George Graham had scored.'

Arsenal's extra-time winner came from the boot of Charlie George, who hit a marvellous shot past Ray Clemence. Arsenal's 2-1 victory gave them a sensational League and Cup double. Match winner George said after the game, 'I knew when I hit that ball that it was the winner. Someone said it was deflected into the goal. That's rubbish. It flew straight as a die from my boot.' Bill Shankly and his team were heartbroken. Tommy Smith remarked, 'I feel so sorry for the boss. He has rebuilt the team and brought us here. Then we can't give him the Cup.'

For Emlyn Hughes it was his first taste of what it was like to play in a major final. Hughes, like several of the Liverpool players, complained after the game that the long-sleeved, heavy, thick shirts that had been designed for them for the final had a draining effect on them. Lots of Liverpool players went down with cramp in a gruelling ninety minutes of play, plus extra time. Hughes concluded that Arsenal were worthy winners and the better team.

Frank McLintock brought the trophy into the Liverpool dressing room for Shankly's team to have a drink of champagne from. Most of the Liverpool team thought this was a nice gesture from the affable Gunners' captain, but some didn't really want to have the trophy that they had just missed out on being paraded in front of them. Emlyn Hughes upset some of the Liverpool party at the traditional post-match banquet when the guest speaker remarked that he was usually invited to the winners' post-match reception. Hughes responded to this remark with a curt 'Well why don't you piss off then?' Some laughed, but the majority thought it was uncalled for.

The players were obviously hurting after failing to win the cup, but generally the Liverpool way was to be magnanimous in victory and defeat. It wouldn't be the last time that Emlyn would upset people with a not very well thought out remark at a Liverpool reception.

CHAPTER 10

'I had a lot of time for Emlyn. He was a terrific player and an inspiration to the team' – Kevin Keegan

Although Liverpool had failed to win a trophy in Emlyn Hughes' first four seasons at Anfield, Bill Shankly's capture of Kevin Keegan in 1971 was in many ways the final piece in the jigsaw that would see the Reds emerge again as the greatest team in the land. Keegan had been a guest of Liverpool at the FA Cup final against Arsenal and after some promising pre-season displays, he forced his way into the Liverpool side at the start of the 1971/72 season. Kevin Keegan was a revelation from the start and, when it came to training, Emlyn Hughes now had a soul mate when it came to wanting to be first at everything. Like Hughes, Keegan had tremendous stamina.

It was around this period that Don Revie made an approach to Bill Shankly in an effort to take Emlyn Hughes to Leeds. Revie offered Peter Lorimer in a straight exchange deal. When the Liverpool boss began to scoff at the mere idea of Hughes leaving Anfield, Revie then offered Lorimer plus a £60,000 fee. Bill Shankly again dismissed Revie's offer out of hand and told the Leeds boss that if he let him have Lorimer, Bremner, Giles, Madeley and Hunter, plus £60,000 he might consider letting Hughes go. Don Revie never discussed the subject of taking Emlyn Hughes to Leeds again with Shankly. It is interesting to note, however, that when he took over from Alf Ramsey as England boss in 1974, Revie selected Hughes only three times before dropping him from the team. A player who he was supposed to rate so highly was then cast into the international wilderness until he was given a recall in 1977.

With Kevin Keegan and John Toshack quickly developing a formidable attacking formation for Liverpool during the 1971/72 campaign, the Reds pressed hard for their first First Division title since 1966. After a slow start, they hit form in a big way at the start of 1972 and went on a 15-game unbeaten run. A 4-0 victory over Everton at Anfield and a 5-0 demolition of Newcastle in March of 1972 confirmed them as championship contenders. Emlyn Hughes scored in both of these victories and it looked like the title could be coming back to Merseyside. Liverpool then suffered a heartbreaking 1-0 defeat at Derby County in the penultimate game of the season. Derby went on to win the First Division for the first time in their history by a single point from Leeds, Liverpool and Manchester City who all finished on the same number of points.

Liverpool had been threatening to win something big for a couple of seasons and Shankly's men would finally bag some silverware the following season. Emlyn Hughes had bagged eight goals during the 1971/72 campaign and was still being used by Shankly as an attacking midfielder. This was only one goal fewer than Kevin Keegan had scored in the League that season, which gives one an idea of just what an eye for goal Hughes had before he dropped back into defence.

The 1972/73 season was a momentous one for Emlyn Hughes and Liverpool, with the First Division title and the UEFA Cup becoming the first trophies that the player had ever won in his career. By now Shankly had added Peter Cormack to his team for a £110,000 fee from Nottingham Forest. Cormack was an excellent acquisition for Liverpool and he took no time in settling into the side.

It was expected to be a two-horse race for the title, with Leeds and Manchester City most bookies' favourites. By Christmas it was Liverpool, however, who were leading the way. Arsenal did briefly take over at the top in February 1973, but Liverpool regained the lead and won the title by three points from the Gunners. Leeds were in third place, seven points behind the Reds. Liverpool clinched the title with a fine 2-0 victory over Leeds. Cormack and Keegan scored the goals with nearly 56,000 packed into Anfield. A jubilant Bill Shankly told the press after the game, 'This is a great team – and it's going to get better. Winning medals makes players improve each year. Now that this team has shown its ability to win something the sky is the limit for them.'

Leeds boss Don Revie was the first into the Liverpool dressing room to congratulate Shankly's team. Revie said, 'All of the Leeds lads are delighted for Liverpool. If we can't win it ourselves then we like to see Liverpool win it.' Revie's team won a lot of new fans at Anfield after the match by lining up to applaud the Reds off the pitch.

The photographs of Emlyn Hughes' beaming face in the following morning's newspapers said everything there was to say about how the kid from Barrow felt about finally becoming a championship winner.

Although the Liverpool boss allowed his team a few celebratory drinks, Shankly's team were due to face Spurs in the second leg of the UEFA Cup semi-final just forty-eight hours later. Liverpool travelled to London, and despite a 2-1 defeat they reached the final on the away goals rule.

The German side Borussia Moenchengladbach stood between Shankly's side and a fabulous European and domestic double. After winning the first game 3-0, Liverpool travelled to Germany and despite a 2-0 defeat won the UEFA Cup 3-2 on aggregate. Bill Shankly had won his first European trophy after nine years of trying. Recalling the second leg in Germany Emlyn Hughes remarked, 'I remember Shanks was wandering up and down the touchline. The tension was obviously too much for him. He was waving his arms and exchanging insults with the Borussia fans, who were howling for him to sit down.'

Emlyn Hughes had another memorable occasion during the 1972/73 season when he was in the England side that travelled up to Hampden Park in February 1973 and beat Scotland 5-0. It was one of the Scots' heaviest defeats to the old enemy on their own turf. The game was Bobby Moore's 100th appearance for his country and Mick Channon, who scored one of the goals, recalled: 'That is a sweet memory because I scored when we turned over Scotland 5-0 in their centenary match on their own ice-covered Hampden Park pitch. If I loved to beat anyone it was them. The Scots have so much passion and I admire them for that, but it didn't stop me hating them when we faced each other.'

The 1973/74 season was destined to be Bill Shankly's last at Liverpool. Emlyn Hughes idolised Shankly and he regarded him as second only to his own father as the greatest man who had ever lived. Liverpool

Emlyn Hughes hugs Bill Shankly after Liverpool clinch the League title in 1973.
Larry Lloyd is also in the photograph.

started the new campaign totally unaware that Shankly had thoughts
in his mind of retiring at the end of it. He had built a fine young team
at Anfield and perhaps success in the European Cup was not now a
forlorn dream.

After beating Luxembourg's Jeunesse D'Esch in the first round of
the competition, Liverpool came up against Red Star Belgrade in the
next round. However, Bill Shankly's European Cup dream came to
an end when Red Star dumped them out of the competition 4-2 on
aggregate. It was destined to be Emlyn Hughes' mentor's last tilt at
the major European prize.

It was during the 1973/74 season that Emlyn Hughes succeeded Tommy Smith as club captain at Liverpool. It was also during this campaign that Hughes began to be employed by Shankly in the centre of the Reds' defence alongside Phil Thompson. Thompson had been brought in to replace the injured Larry Lloyd early in 1974 and formed such a good partnership with Hughes that the Liverpool boss stuck with them until the end of the season. Hughes was still capable of playing the attacking midfield role, as his seven goals in the League during the 1972/73 season confirms. At centre-back, however, he looked totally at home, almost like Anfield's own version of Franz Beckenbauer at the heart of the Liverpool defence.

Liverpool failed in their attempt to retain their League title, losing out to Leeds United, but in the FA Cup it was a glorious end to Shankly's managerial reign at the club. Hughes and Thompson at the heart of the Liverpool defence had a superb day out at Wembley, as did the whole of Shankly's team. Goals from Heighway and Keegan, who scored two, gave Liverpool an emphatic 3-0 victory over Newcastle United.

Emlyn Hughes proudly climbed the steps to the royal box to collect the FA Cup, his first trophy as captain. As Princess Anne handed Hughes the cup, the confirmed royalist later described the moment as one of the greatest of his life.

With his first trophy in the bag as captain, Emlyn Hughes turned up for pre-season training with the rest of the Liverpool squad in a positive frame of mind. Their display in the FA Cup final against Newcastle had been sensational and Shankly had built a team that looked like they would dominate the English game for years. As the team got ready for their first training session of the season at Melwood on a warm summer morning in July 1974, their manager delivered a bombshell. He walked into the dressing room and confirmed what the local news station and newspapers had been reporting. Bill Shankly had retired from football.

A delighted Emlyn Hughes holds the FA Cup after Liverpool's victory over Newcastle in the 1974 final. Liverpool goalkeeper Ray Clemence is alongside Hughes.

CHAPTER 11

'Mike Pejic doesn't effin' well smile. I'm not having him in my team if he doesn't smile. I'll get Alec Lindsay in' – Caretaker England boss Joe Mercer to new England captain Emlyn Hughes.

The summer of 1974 saw Emlyn Hughes' great mentor, Bill Shankly, decide to retire from football. Earlier in the year, Hughes was also saddened to see another great manager, Sir Alf Ramsey, lose his job as England boss. Hughes thought the world of Ramsey, and Rodney Marsh, who was a teammate of the Liverpool skipper in the national side on several occasions, once remarked, 'If Alf Ramsey had told Emlyn Hughes to kick Denis Law in the head during a game I'm sure he would have done. He thought that much of Alf.'

The end came for Ramsey when England failed to beat Poland in a qualifying game at Wembley for the 1974 World Cup finals. The Poland match took place on 17 October 1973. England had lost the away game in Poland 2-0 and needed to beat them to progress to the finals alongside the other qualifiers from their group, Italy.

The Polish goalkeeper, Jan Tomaszewski, who Brian Clough, speaking on television, had dubbed 'a clown', had an inspired game and England could only manage a 1-1 draw. They were out of the World Cup and Emlyn Hughes was destined never to compete in the world's greatest football tournament.

Sir Alf Ramsey lasted for just two more games before being sacked. Emlyn Hughes remarked in his autobiography, 'The Poland match was really Sir Alf's do or die game. When the inquests were over, the daggers that had been aimed at Sir Alf's back for some time now went straight in.'

Merseyside football great Joe Mercer took over as caretaker-manager and immediately made Emlyn Hughes the new England captain. Bill Shankly's outrageous prophesy to a startled Lancashire policeman way back in 1967 that the future captain of England was sitting in the back of the car had been proved correct.

Joe Mercer knew that the England job would only be on a temporary basis and at his first press conference the smiling Mercer remarked, 'I'll just tell the players to go out and enjoy themselves. I'll just hold the reins for a few weeks, but I don't want the job on a permanent basis.'

England went on a summer tour of Eastern Europe and played games against Germany, Bulgaria and Yugoslavia. Emlyn Hughes had captained the England team in the 1974 Home International Championships and he retained his captaincy for the East European tour. Joe Mercer was a breath of fresh air as England boss and even dropped one player, Mike Pejic, from the tour because he didn't smile enough. Pejic was replaced at left-back by Liverpool's Alec Lindsay. Mick Channon recalled in his autobiography that it was a joy to play for Mercer. He said: 'He was brilliant, I don't think anyone else could have done the job that he did. Joe had a tremendous happy go lucky attitude towards it and we got some great results for him with a draw in Leipzig, a win in Sofia and another draw in Belgrade. He kept the team together through some testing times. Joe was a lovely romantic when it came to football.'

England returned from their summer tour unbeaten and Emlyn Hughes looked like he was destined to become Bobby Moore's natural successor as England captain for many years to come. Hughes' international aspirations were to receive a severe shock, however, when Don Revie succeeded Joe Mercer as England manager. Mercer had only been holding the fort for the expected appointment of Revie and in July 1974 the former Leeds United manager took over the national team.

Hughes captained the England side for the remainder of 1974. England defeated Czechoslovakia 3-0 at Wembley, Colin Bell scoring two of the goals, and then drew with Portugal 0-0. Emlyn Hughes was then unceremoniously dumped by Revie, not just from the captaincy but from the England team altogether for the text two internationals, without ever being given a proper explanation by the new England boss.

At the time Hughes was developing into one of the finest defenders not just in England but also in Europe. His partnership with Phil Thompson at Anfield had looked exceptional and it had looked to be only a matter of time before the young Liverpool defender would be joining Hughes at the heart of the England defence. Alan Ball took over from Hughes as England skipper for the game against West Germany at Wembley in March 1975, which the home side won 2-0. Ball then led England to a 5-0 victory over Cyprus. Hughes was then selected by Revie for the games against Cyprus and Northern Ireland.

It was on the eve of England's next Home International against Wales that Revie called Hughes to his room to inform him that he no longer figured in his England plans. Hughes left the room shell-shocked. When he returned to his room to tell Kevin Keegan about Revie's decision his Liverpool teammate thought it was just another Hughes wind-up and refused to believe him. Emlyn Hughes was just twenty-seven years old and at the peak of his form but, for the time being, his international career had come to an end.

What had driven Don Revie to cast Hughes into the international wilderness was the subject of much conjecture. Don Revie obviously wanted to stamp his own mark on the team and he had even left out Kevin Keegan for the game against Wales, as he had also done for the Portugal match which had been Revie's second as manager. Liverpool and Leeds had been involved in some stormy encounters over the years, but it is doubtful that Revie would have held that against Emlyn Hughes. They might have been the scenes of some of the bitterest games in English football during the 1960s and early 1970s, but Leeds and Liverpool always had a deep respect for each other.

Bill Shankly, a man not prone to telling fibs, had mentioned himself in his autobiography that Don Revie was desperate to sign Emlyn Hughes at the start of the 1970s. Now Revie didn't rate him. Whatever the reasons, Hughes no longer figured in the new England manager's plans and he returned to Anfield after the 1975 Home International

Championships determined to bring further success to Liverpool and prove Don Revie wrong.

Emlyn Hughes would have discussed his dropping from the England team not only with Bob Paisley back at Liverpool but also with his old mentor Bill Shankly. Hughes still continued to visit Shankly most afternoons after training and on one occasion the great man almost revealed his real reason for leaving Liverpool. Emlyn Hughes recalled in an interview: 'It's impossible to know exactly what his reasons were, but I used to keep in touch with him after he had retired and I went to see him every day after training. One day he asked me if I wanted a drink and I said, "Yes please, I'll have a cup of tea." "No," he said, "I mean a proper drink. I want to tell you the real reason why I left Liverpool." I said, "No boss, you don't have to, I don't want to know," but he insisted. He asked Ness to go and get us a couple of whiskies and we retired to the front room of his house. Ness brought the drinks through and just as we settled down the doorbell rang. It was his daughter with the two grandkids and that was that. The moment had gone. He never did tell me and I never asked him.' As well as Bill Shankly departing the Anfield scene it was also during this period that Emlyn Hughes lost the man who had guided his football career with such dedication throughout his life. Fred 'Ginger' Hughes died after a long illness one evening while his son was giving his all for Liverpool away at Manchester United in the mid-1970s. Without Fred's relentless drive and enthusiasm on behalf of his son it is doubtful that Emlyn's professional football career would have taken off at all.

CHAPTER 12

'There were no superstars at Liverpool, they treated everyone the same, from the young apprentice to the England captain' – Emlyn Hughes.

Bob Paisley's first season in charge at Liverpool failed to produce any silverware. The Reds were pipped to the 1975 First Division title by Derby County by just two points.

In Europe Liverpool were fancied to go all the way in the European Cup-Winners' Cup, particularly after thrashing Norwegian side Stromgodset 11-0 in their opening game. In the very next round, however, Ferencvaros put the Reds out on the away goals rule after holding Liverpool to a 1-1 draw at Anfield and 0-0 on their own ground.

Everyone knew that it would take Bob Paisley a little time to get accustomed to becoming Shankly's successor at Anfield. He had almost won the title in his first season at the helm and he made no mistake a year later. With new names in the Liverpool squad such as Phil Neal, Ray Kennedy, Jimmy Case, Terry McDermott, David Fairclough and Joey Jones, Paisley had built a formidable outfit. A lot of the Shankly boys such as Tommy Smith, Ian Callaghan, Ray Clemence, Kevin Keegan and Steve Heighway were still forming the backbone of the team. Emlyn Hughes and Phil Thompson had formed an outstanding defensive partnership for the Reds and John Toshack was still knocking in important goals.

One of Liverpool's best displays of the 1975/76 season came when Toshack scored the winner in an outstanding 1-0 defeat of Spanish giants Barcelona in the away leg of the UEFA Cup semi-final. Liverpool's display in the Nou Camp had the rest of Europe now

noticing that Paisley's team had the potential to become the dominant
force in the European game. Barcelona had the outstanding Cruyff
and Neeskens in their team, but Hughes and Thompson gave the
Dutch stars few chances to cause the Liverpool defence any moments
of anxiety. Bob Paisley had not instructed his defence to man mark
Cruyff and Neeskens and Emlyn Hughes told the press after the game,
'We can't play that way. We are far happier letting teams come at us
and playing our own game.'

A delighted Bob Paisley remarked, 'That was a perfect night's work.
I couldn't have planned it better. It leaves us in control and Barcelona
have an almighty task at Anfield. Our defence took everything they
had to offer and our midfield were superb. Even after twelve years
playing in Europe, this is one of our greatest victories.'

Emlyn Hughes, standing next to Paisley at the press conference,
concluded, 'We were tremendous, I'm just disappointed we didn't
score two or three more goals. We should have.'

Liverpool went on to hold Barcelona to a 1-1 draw in the return leg
at Anfield, Phil Thompson scoring a rare goal for the Reds. They had
reached their first European final under the management of Paisley and
the captaincy of Hughes. Their opponents were Belgian side Bruges.
Both manager and skipper were proving themselves to be quite formidable exponents of the art of leadership. Steve Heighway remarked
in his autobiography that Emlyn Hughes never thought twice about
giving a teammate a telling-off if he thought warranted it. Heighway
said, 'We were playing a European tie in Bucharest and at half-time
Emlyn gave me a rollicking because I'd opted for a shot when I could
have passed to him. He obviously reckoned he was better placed for
having a crack at goal and he'd had a go at me on the pitch about it.
When he took up the matter again in the dressing room I began to
argue the toss with him. His reaction was short and to the point: "Who
the hell do you think you're talking to?" Emlyn was captain and he
was reminding me of it. He demanded respect and while at the time
I thought he was making a stupid fuss about nothing, I have come to
realise since that the skipper must have the respect of his teammates.'

In the League campaign Liverpool were involved in a tight struggle
with surprise package Queens Park Rangers for the title during the

The most successful manager in Liverpool's history, Bob Paisley. Emlyn Hughes captained two of Paisley's teams to European Cup wins in 1977 and 1978.

1975/76 season. Although Emlyn Hughes was now captain, he was still not averse to becoming involved in the occasional flare-up with members of the opposition. During one game against Leeds United Hughes walked off at half-time with a cut eye. Joey Jones was a new recruit to the Liverpool side and in his autobiography he recalled the incident: 'Allan Clarke stamped on my foot before running off. I lost my head and went after him slinging punches wildly. Next minute Billy Bremner came up to me, warning me off. Leeds players stuck together, playing and fighting for each other. It calmed down, although I do remember Emlyn having a go at Clarke in the tunnel at half-time after Clarke had cut Emlyn's eye. "I'll get you Clarky," he was screeching in his high pitched voice'.

Liverpool travelled to Wolves for their final game of the season needing a win to be certain of depriving Queens Park Rangers of their first ever First Division title. The game took place on a Tuesday evening early in May 1976. Wolves needed to win to have a chance of staying in the First Division and for the first hour of the game the League title looked destined for Loftus Road. Wolves' thirteenth-minute goal from Steve Kindon meant that Queens Park Rangers would end the season as champions if the Midlands club could protect their lead until full-time. Gradually, Liverpool's midfield began to take control of the game and Kevin Keegan equalised after seventy-six minutes. Further goals from John Toshack and Ray Kennedy sealed Wolves' fate. Liverpool were champions, Wolverhampton Wanderers were relegated. An ecstatic Emlyn Hughes celebrated with his teammates in the dressing-room at Molineux and told the press, 'On behalf of all the lads I want to thank the boss. We won the title for him.'

Liverpool's title success by just one point from Queens Park Rangers delighted Reds fans, but the sporting press could not hide the fact that they would have been delighted if the London team had succeeded in denying Liverpool their fourth championship in twelve years. *The Times* commented: 'It is two years since Bill Shankly left them and some panache went with him into retirement. Their image outside Merseyside is unexciting and even unpopular. Liverpool are part of the establishment now with results reading like an insurance company's statement of profits. Only through defeat or scandal do they make the headlines and, for better or worse, nothing so vulgar is allowed to take root at Anfield. Aggressive and uncompromising at home, strong and conservative on their travels, football is learning to hate them for it.' It is interesting to note that almost thirty years later the same type of barbed comments are now being penned about Jose Mourinho's successful Chelsea side.

Whether universally acclaimed or not, Bob Paisley's side continued to fill the Anfield trophy cabinet with silverware when they defeated Bruges over two legs to take the 1976 UEFA Cup. Goals from Kennedy, Case and Keegan gave Liverpool a 3-2 victory after a thrilling first leg at Anfield. A 1-1 draw in Bruges saw Emlyn Hughes lifting his first European trophy as captain.

Bill Shankly, Bob Paisley and Manchester United boss Tommy Docherty pictured together at Anfield in the 1970s. Emlyn Hughes played under just two managers at Liverpool, Shankly and Paisley.

There was further good news for the Liverpool skipper in 1976 when Don Revie included him in the England side to take on Italy in Rome. Hughes had been in outstanding form since Revie had discarded him from the England set-up, but he was still surprised to receive a call from the England manager to inform him of his selection. Emlyn Hughes almost blew his recall, however, when two years of pent-up anger exploded down the phone to Revie. Hughes had been tipped off by Bob Paisley earlier in the day that Revie would be contacting him. Paisley had stressed to Hughes that he must keep his cool when Revie called. Emlyn Hughes' exemption from the international set-up had obviously been a sore point with him for some time and everyone at Anfield knew about his dislike of Don Revie.

When the call came Hughes had downed a few glasses of champagne to celebrate and the alcohol had loosened his tongue. He told the England boss exactly what he thought of him and was well on the way to talking himself out of an international recall. When he put the phone down he came to his senses and called Bill Shankly to obtain Revie's home phone number. Eventually the matter was resolved with the England boss welcoming Hughes back into the England squad when they had a get-together in London before the 13 October 1976 World Cup qualifier against Finland. Hughes was not selected for this game, but Revie picked him for the next World Cup qualifier against Italy in Rome a month later.

Emlyn Hughes was destined never to really have a good working relationship with Don Revie. Hughes did acknowledge that when he met Revie a few years after he resigned from the England job the former Leeds boss apologised for the shoddy way that he treated the Liverpool captain when he dumped him from the England team.

CHAPTER 13

'Emlyn Hughes was the heart of that outstanding Liverpool team of the 1970s. He seemed to grow whenever he pulled on the Liverpool shirt' – Steve Coppell.

Emlyn Hughes' career may have failed to hit the heights as an England player, but at Liverpool in the 1970s it became one glorious triumph after another.

Although Bill Shankly was never in awe of the legendary status surrounding the European Cup, he had always held a firm conviction that Liverpool would have been the first English side to have won the trophy but for some outrageous refereeing decisions in the second leg of their 1965 semi-final against Inter Milan in Italy. In the 1976/77 season Bob Paisley guided Liverpool to their first European Cup success with Emlyn Hughes becoming the first Reds skipper to hold the trophy aloft.

Liverpool's path to the final began against Crusaders, the Northern Ireland Champions. The Reds won the tie against the Irish part-timers 7-0 on aggregate. Trabzonspor of Turkey came next and were comfortably accounted for 3-1 over the two legs.

Liverpool's most severe test came in the next round when they were pitched against the champions of France, St Etienne. The quarter-final tie has gone down in Anfield folklore as probably the greatest European match that the ground has ever staged. Liverpool were 1-0 down from the first leg in France, but when Kevin Keegan put the Reds 1-0 up after just two minutes of the return leg at Anfield, Paisley's boys were expected to romp to a convincing victory.

The St Etienne danger man Bathenay put his team back in front on aggregate early in the second half with a fabulous goal from thirty yards out. Liverpool now needed to score twice to progress to the semi-finals, the away goals rule meaning that the odds were now stacked heavily in St Etienne's favour.

Ray Kennedy gave Liverpool hope with a low drive from the edge of the penalty area past the away team's goalkeeper, Jurcovic, after fifty-eight minutes. The Reds continued to press for number three, the goal that would put them through, and it came six minutes from time from David Fairclough. Ray Kennedy set up one of the most famous goals in Liverpool's history when he scooped the ball over the French team's defence for Fairclough to latch on to it and place the ball past the St Etienne goalkeeper from ten yards out. Anfield erupted and Liverpool were through.

After a momentous night at Anfield, Emlyn Hughes told the *Liverpool Echo*: 'For the first ten minutes they were the noisiest crowd that I have ever played in front of. We got so much on top that you could hardly hear them at all. When St Etienne scored we didn't panic because the Liverpool adage has always been don't go mad at it, running around like lunatics to turn things round. Your chance will come. When we finally got that third goal we all felt that we now had a great chance of winning our first European Cup.'

Bob Paisley and his Liverpool team were delighted to be drawn against Swiss champions Zurich in the semi-finals. They were undoubtedly the weakest team left in the competition and Liverpool's progress to the final looked a formality. Emlyn Hughes voiced the sentiments of all the Liverpool team when he recalled: 'We were praying we would get Zurich. We were bombing then and we felt that if we were ever going to win the European Cup that would be our year. Zurich were frightened to death of us. You could tell by the way they played. We were virtually unstoppable.' Liverpool duly saw off the Swiss Champions, but in the final they would come up against much stronger opposition in the shape of German Champions Borussia Moenchengladbach.

Before the European Cup final was due to take place, Paisley's team had to face neighbours Everton in an FA Cup semi-final and also see off the challenges of Manchester City and Ipswich Town in order to retain their First Division title.

The game against Everton at Maine Road, Manchester remains one of the most contentious Merseyside derby encounters to this day. With the teams drawing 2-2, referee Clive Thomas disallowed what looked an Everton winner in the closing stages by Bryan Hamilton. The game ended in a draw, but in the replay four days later Liverpool romped to an easy 3-0 victory. They were through to another FA Cup final and their opponents were Manchester United.

Although Everton had been unlucky not to progress in the first game of the 1977 semi-final, Emlyn Hughes had in the main always enjoyed fairly good fortune during his time at Liverpool in derby games. His best performance was probably back in March 1973 when he scored Liverpool's two goals in a 2-0 win at Goodison Park. Evertonians would, at a push, undoubtedly have acknowledged that Hughes was a fine footballer in his heyday at Liverpool, a player that they would have loved Harry Catterick to have signed for the Blues before Bill Shankly snapped him up from Blackpool in 1967.

The confidence that so endeared Emlyn to Liverpudlians however, sometimes came across as arrogance to the blue half of Merseyside. He once stated in an interview for Brian Barwick and Gerald Sinstadt's book *The Great Derbies* that during the 1970s Liverpool's routine victories over Everton had become almost monotonous: 'For the first three years I was at Anfield, the derbies were fabulous – unbelievable. Up to 1970 we were both, us and Everton, always at the top, always doing well in cups and such like and the derbies dominated the whole outlook of the city. After 1970, I've got to be honest and say that, for me, they went flat. I played that many games against them without being on the losing side and we knew we wouldn't be. The truth was they weren't really opposition for us and it got almost embarrassing when you knew that you were going to win every time.' From the early 1970s through to leaving Liverpool in 1979, the Reds' skipper was never on a losing side against the Blues.

With their place booked at Wembley for the 1977 FA Cup final against Manchester United, Liverpool now set their sights on retaining the League title. Manchester City pushed Paisley's team all the way for the championship, but a crucial 2-1 victory over their Manchester rivals in April put the Reds in the driving seat.

With Liverpool fighting for three major trophies, Bob Paisley was asked about fatigue affecting his team. Paisley replied: 'The only players who go on about tiredness after so many games are those who don't win anything. My team get tired, but it is no problem playing twice a week when you are playing as well as us.' Victories over Manchester City and Leeds in the final weeks of the 1976/77 campaign meant that if Liverpool could take a single point at Anfield against West Ham in their final home game of the season, then the first leg of an historic treble would be in the bag.

Queues started to form at Anfield, which in those days was not an all-ticket ground for major League games, from 8.00 a.m. for the vital game against West Ham. The game was also, incidentally, destined to be Kop idol Kevin Keegan's last League game for the Reds. The game was actually something of an anticlimax, with West Ham holding Liverpool to a 0-0 draw. Paisley's team had obtained the point they needed, but a series of fine saves from young West Ham goalkeeper, Mervyn Day, denied the Reds the opportunity to take the title in style with an emphatic victory. As Emlyn Hughes and his team paraded the First Division trophy around Anfield, Bob Paisley joined them on the pitch for the victory parade. Paisley was proving to be an outstanding manager and Emlyn Hughes an inspirational captain.

The FA Cup final was next on the agenda and Hughes told the press that Liverpool had barely been able to draw breath with vital matches cropping up every few days in the final weeks of the season. Hughes said, 'It was not until the FA Cup semi-final against Everton that the lads really began to think about Wembley. With so much at stake in every game, they've all been like cup-ties to us. Taking each game one at a time, we've tended to overlook the prospect of a glamour day at Wembley.'

Liverpool set off for Wembley in confident mood. Manchester United had finished ten points behind them in the First Division and the Merseysiders knew that an incredible treble was in their grasp. Bob Paisley decided to leave new wonder kid David Fairclough out of the Wembley team. David Johnson also kept Ian Callaghan out of the starting line-up. Paisley was asked on the eve of the game why Fairclough had not been included and the Liverpool boss replied,

'Picking David Fairclough to charge around on that lush Wembley turf would have been like committing Hari Kari.'

Norman Fox of *The Times* in his Wembley preview paid a handsome tribute to Liverpool's skipper when he remarked, 'Emlyn Hughes dispenses generous quantities of enthusiasm as well as making up for the errors of others.' Hughes' fine positional play in the Liverpool defence had never been more apparent than in the momentous 1976/77 season.

Although Liverpool were the firm favourites, Tommy Docherty's Manchester United ended the Reds' dreams of the treble with a 2-1 victory in the FA Cup final. Stuart Pearson opened the scoring for United when Ray Clemence made a rare mistake by allowing the striker's weak shot to slip under his body. Jimmy Case equalised minutes later when he crashed a shot past Stepney for a fabulous goal. United's winner was something of a fluke when Lou Macari mis-hit his shot which was going out of play before it cannoned off Jimmy Greenhoff and looped over Clemence's head into the goal. Whether a freak goal or not, they all count and the FA Cup went to Old Trafford. Bob Paisley and his team were heartbroken, but had only a few days to lift their spirits before the European Cup final the following week against Borussia Moenchengladbach in Rome.

It is interesting to note that at the end of the game as Bob Paisley and his dejected team trooped off the Wembley pitch, the United fans actually struck up a chant of 'Liverpool, Liverpool'. The chances of that happening in the modern game, when the rivalry between Liverpool and United verges on total hatred, would be slim indeed.

CHAPTER 14

'You wouldn't say Emlyn was shy, on or off the pitch. Other people didn't like him, but he was always all right to me. All that really matters is that Emlyn contributed on the pitch. You can't expect eighteen or twenty guys in a dressing room to all be best friends' – Kenny Dalglish.

By the time the Liverpool team set off on the journey to Rome for the 1977 European Cup final, Bob Paisley, Joe Fagan, Ronnie Moran and the rest of the Anfield boot room staff had them raring to go. Their unfortunate defeat against Manchester United might have ended their dreams of an unprecedented treble, but they were determined to bring the European Cup back to Anfield for the first time. Their opponents Borussia Moenchengladbach were a formidable outfit with star names such as Vogts, Bonhof, Simonsen and Heynckes in their team.

Liverpool's travelling supporters virtually took over the Olympic Stadium and Emlyn Hughes and his team knew they didn't dare return to Anfield without the European Cup. 'When we walked out and saw how many had travelled to Rome you could not even contemplate losing,' said Hughes.

Liverpool won their first European Cup after a stunning 3-1 victory over the German champions. Terry McDermott, Tommy Smith and Phil Neal with a penalty were the Reds' goalscorers on a night of triumph for Liverpool Football Club. Emlyn Hughes proudly lifted the trophy and the celebrations in Rome and back home on Merseyside went on well into the night.

Kevin Keegan was playing his last game for Liverpool before signing for German club Hamburg. Keegan had a fine game against Berti Vogts, who at the time was regarded as the outstanding German defender of his day. Ian Callaghan had been brought back into the side in place of David Johnson after being dropped by Paisley for the FA Cup final. Callaghan and Smith were veterans of Bill Shankly's first forays into Europe back in 1965 and finally to win a European Cup was a dream come true.

For Emlyn Hughes, captaining the Liverpool team to a European Cup victory crowned his football career. Apart from Liverpool winning the League and European Cup, Emlyn was also voted the Footballer of the Year in 1977 and later in the year he would win his fiftieth England cap against Italy in a World Cup qualifier. Despite his public image as a very self-confident individual, Emlyn Hughes displayed a great degree of modesty when he said of winning the Footballer of the Year accolade, 'To be fair, I got the votes because I lifted the trophies, not because I was a better player than the other Liverpool lads.'

Liverpool returned home after becoming the first English winners of the European Cup since Manchester United in 1968 to a heroes' welcome. The streets of Liverpool were lined with thousands of well-wishers decked in the colours of Liverpool – and some even in the blue of Everton. Evertonians would have loved for it to have been their Goodison Park heroes who had brought the European Cup back to Merseyside for the first time instead of their rivals from across Stanley Park. The blue half of Merseyside was envious, but in some ways proud that their fellow Scousers had brought pride to Liverpool. Half of Paisley's team were local lads anyway. When the Liverpool team set off to parade the European Cup through the streets of Liverpool on an open-top bus, some of the triumphant squad on the bus were slightly taken aback to see a fair number of Evertonians applauding them as they drove past! Local lads such as Callaghan, Smith, Case and McDermott were probably not surprised at all; this was Liverpool and not Glasgow, after all.

Unfortunately, Emlyn Hughes failed to take in the fact that Evertonians were part of the multitude of fans giving them a heroes' welcome as they drove through Liverpool. When the team arrived at Liverpool Art Gallery, Emlyn Hughes, as team captain, was called upon to say a few words. Emlyn had for years listened to his great mentor

Bill Shankly mocking Everton Football Club, but the difference was
that Shankly never attempted to ridicule Evertonians. He would talk
football for hours with both Liverpool and Everton fans. After his
retirement at Liverpool he was always made welcome at Everton's
training ground at Bellefield and also at Goodison Park by both the
club staff and the supporters. When Emlyn Hughes began to sing
'Liverpool are magic, Everton are tragic' on the steps of Liverpool
Art Gallery it was heard not just by those present, but by millions
watching on television.

Bob Paisley and the rest of the Liverpool squad cringed. Emlyn
Hughes had been prone to moments of eccentric behaviour throughout his Anfield career – he was, after all, 'Crazy Horse' – but spouting
those words into a microphone in front of the television cameras was
deeply insulting to the blue half of Merseyside.

A repentant Emlyn Hughes made an apology the next day on television, but the damage was done. Over the years, football fans who
had the pleasure of meeting Emlyn Hughes after his retirement from
the game have been unanimous in their opinions that he was one of
the most amiable ex-football stars that they had ever met. He would
talk football for hours, particularly with Evertonians. Back in 1977,
however, on the steps of Liverpool Art Gallery, Emlyn did himself
no favours when it came to public relations on Merseyside. Although
they would remain a side capable of challenging the best in the First
Division until their demise in the Premiership years of the 1990s,
Evertonians didn't need reminding after Liverpool's 1977 European
Cup triumph just how far they had suddenly fallen behind their Anfield
neighbours.

Emlyn Hughes' 'Everton are tragic' remarks were seen as rubbing
their noses in it. In later years when Emlyn was asked about the incident he freely admitted that it was the biggest mistake of his Liverpool
career.

CHAPTER 15

'Emlyn Hughes was still a top-class player when Liverpool sold him. The standards that Liverpool set, however, were higher than at other clubs. His past record counted for nothing. I found this chilling' – Alan Hansen.

In July 1977 Emlyn Hughes, like a great many in football, was not unduly concerned to hear the news that Don Revie had resigned as England manager. Revie had been a brilliant manager at Leeds, but his England days had been a failure. He had tried to run the England set-up like he had at Leeds, but his parlour games and in-depth dossiers on the opposition were laughed at by England's elite when they came together for internationals.

In today's more regimented game, the Revie approach probably wouldn't have looked out of place at all, but back in the 1970s it was acceptable for players to wind down after (sometimes before) a game with a night on the town. Mick Channon was an England regular during the Revie era and said, 'Don wanted the England team to be like his boys at Leeds. He was trying to do everything right, but just having the mickey taken out of him. I don't think he could trust anyone, he thought everyone was out to do him.'

Revie's successor as England manager was West Ham legend Ron Greenwood. England had a slim chance to qualify for the 1978 World Cup finals when Greenwood took over. Failure to knock in more than two goals against minnows Luxembourg meant that Italy were now virtual certainties to top England's group and deprive them of a place in the finals.

Don Revie had stated before he left the England job to take over as coach of the United Arab Emirates team that he wanted to base

England's style of play on Liverpool's. Revie never stayed long enough
to try out this course of action, but new boss Ron Greenwood included
six Liverpool players, plus the recently departed Kevin Keegan, for
his first game in charge. England failed to impress in a 0-0 draw
with Switzerland and by the time Greenwood's team played Italy in
November only Clemence, Hughes and Neal were still in the team.

Nonetheless, Emlyn Hughes was impressed by Ron Greenwood
and the better atmosphere that now radiated from the England camp.
One of West Ham's 1966 World Cup heroes, Geoff Hurst, visited
the England camp during one of Greenwood's first training sessions
and was immediately struck by how down to earth the Liverpool contingent were. Hurst recalled, 'Even the Liverpool players who had won
so much were eager to learn from Ron Greenwood. I was particularly
impressed by them and it helped me understand why they had won so
much. I already knew Callaghan, Clemence and Hughes and what I
noticed when they were together was how down to earth they were.
There were no stars and none of the huge egos that some carry around
today. I remember Emlyn Hughes, who had played under Alf, saying
that Ron had brought back the family atmosphere to the squad.'

At Anfield Liverpool, the reigning champions of Europe, replaced
Kevin Keegan at the start of the 1977/78 season with Kenny Dalglish.
Keegan took some replacing, but Dalglish had a sensational career at
Liverpool and Emlyn Hughes once said that only Dalglish or Trevor
Francis were good enough to have taken Keegan's place. Indeed,
Hughes went on to proclaim, 'If anything Kenny was even better than
Kevin when it came to all-round team play.' When it came to replacing
key players in their team, Liverpool rarely got it wrong. Emlyn Hughes
once said, 'They had the knack of choosing good players. Of course,
they got the pick of the bunch because everyone wanted to come to
Liverpool. They rarely made mistakes in the transfer market.'

Another Scot who was destined to become an Anfield legend, Alan
Hansen, was also now in Paisley's squad. Hansen would ultimately
replace Emlyn Hughes at the heart of the Liverpool defence, but he
did not become a regular until the following season.

Although Kenny Dalglish slotted into Kevin Keegan's place in the
Liverpool side as though he had been an Anfield regular for years, the

Emlyn Hughes holds the European Cup aloft after
Liverpool's victory in the 1977 final in Rome.

Reds failed to retain their First Division title in his first season at the
club. Brian Clough's Nottingham Forest won the League title by seven
points from Paisley's team, but in the European Cup Emlyn Hughes
had the honour of lifting the trophy for a second time.

With the final of the 1977/78 European Cup being played at Wembley,
the Liverpool team were determined to retain their trophy at the home
of English football. Liverpool coasted through the competition account-
ing for Dynamo Dresden, Benfica and Borussia Moenchengladbach
with the minimum of fuss. Emlyn Hughes even found time to pop up
and score a goal against Benfica in Liverpool's impressive 2-1 victory
at the Stadium of Light. Scoring goals for the Reds had become, at
this stage of his Anfield career, a rare occurrence for Hughes, with his
days as a marauding midfielder now well behind him.

Liverpool met Belgian champions Bruges in the Wembley final. A
fabulous goal from Kenny Dalglish in an otherwise uneventful game
gave Liverpool a 1-0 victory. Bruges had come to Wembley in a totally
negative frame of mind and hoped to win the game with a breakaway
after soaking up Liverpool pressure. Emlyn Hughes and his jubilant
teammates didn't really care how they won it, as long as the European
Cup stayed at Anfield.

Emlyn Hughes spoke in later years about how he felt on that May
evening at Wembley in 1978: 'When Liverpool won the European Cup
in 1978, I remember looking and seeing that huge trophy glittering in

Emlyn Hughes and his Liverpool teammates Phil Neal and Terry McDemott on
their way to a World Cup qualifier against Luxembourg in October 1977. England
won 2-0, Ray Kennedy and Paul Mariner scoring the goals.

the light from the floodlights. I wondered whether I would be able to
lift it. I was in such a high plane of excitement that I really believed I
could have lifted Red Rum above my head that night.'

If Liverpool boss Bob Paisley was regarded as immortal after capturing the cup for the first time for the Reds in 1977, to lead his team to
a second consecutive European Cup cemented his place alongside Bill
Shankly as an Anfield god. Emlyn Hughes said of Paisley, 'In terms of
winning trophies and building two separate teams to win European
Cups, Bob was the greatest. His greatest quality was knowing his players and knowing what he could get out of them.'

Apart from Dalglish and Hansen, another brilliant Scot also became a European Cup winner for the first time. Graeme Souness had joined the club for £352,000 from Middlesbrough in January 1978 and Emlyn Hughes once paid Souness this tribute: 'When I was at Liverpool we had some brilliant players, but we only ever had three gems, Keegan, Dalglish and Souness. They were the only players at Anfield when I was there that you would call world class.'

Apart from retaining their European Cup, Liverpool finished runners-up in the League and narrowly failed to win the only trophy that Emlyn Hughes never won at Anfield, the League Cup. Nottingham Forest beat them 1-0 in the final after a replay.

Emlyn Hughes began the 1978/79 campaign knowing that his days at Liverpool could soon be drawing to a close. His Anfield career had been built on superb fitness and picking up very few injuries. However, in a 1978/79 encounter against Spurs, Hughes sustained a knee injury that would dog him until his playing days came to an end. Hughes played only 16 League games for Liverpool in his final season at the club. Although it was enough games for him to qualify for yet another League Championship medal, his fourth at the club, it was not ultimately a satisfactory farewell season for the Anfield legend. Apart from his injury problems, he was in the Liverpool side that were unexpectedly dumped out of the FA Cup by Manchester United in a semi-final replay at Goodison Park in April 1979. Hughes had enjoyed many triumphant moments against Everton at Goodison during his Anfield career. Defeat against United when only one step away from what would have been a farewell appearance for his beloved Liverpool in an FA Cup final at Wembley hit Hughes hard.

It was destined to be Emlyn Hughes' final appearance for Liverpool and a Jimmy Greenhoff goal ended Liverpool's Wembley dreams. Hughes' last League game for the Reds had come a week earlier in a 2-0 victory over Ipswich at Anfield. After 657 appearances in the red of Liverpool, Bob Paisley told Emlyn Hughes in the summer of 1979 that Wolverhampton Wanderers manager John Barnwell had approached the club and that Wolves' £90,000 bid for his services had been accepted. Hughes was offered a three-year deal by Barnwell, but because of his persistent knee trouble declined the three-year option

Liverpool legends Bob Paisley and Joe Fagan. Both kept the trophies coming to
Anfield on a regular basis.

and signed for just one season. Only the great Ian Callaghan had ever
played more games for Liverpool than Emlyn Hughes.

Emlyn's father Fred, the man who had guided his son's career as
a youngster, had died a few years prior to Liverpool's glory days in
Europe. There is little doubt however that he would have been delighted
that his son was now ending his First Division career at such a famous
old club as Wolverhampton Wanderers. Wolves also came with a high
recommendation from Hughes' mentor, Bill Shankly.

CHAPTER 16

'The League Cup was the one trophy Emlyn hadn't won at Liverpool. This was his last shot and he gave it everything' – Andy Gray on Wolves' League Cup victory in 1980.

Although Emlyn Hughes was now a Wolverhampton Wanderers player he continued to live in his Liverpool home at Formby with his wife Barbara and two young children, Emma and Emlyn junior.

Emlyn Hughes' first game for Wolves was against Derby County on 22 August 1979. Wolves won 1-0 and Hughes had a sound game. His troublesome knee had stood up well to the rigours of First Division football and Hughes actually completed 35 League games for Wolves during the 1979/80 season .

Apart from Hughes, Wolves had several other players who were reaching the veteran stage in their careers, such as Willie Carr, Kenny Hibbitt and John Richards. Andy Gray had also recently signed for Wolves. Gray actually phoned Bill Shankly to ask his advice when he found out that a number of clubs were after his signature. Without hesitation Shankly told him to join up with Emlyn Hughes at Wolves. The former Liverpool boss rated Wolves manager John Barnwell highly.

Andy Gray got on well with Hughes at Wolves and found him an excellent teammate. Gray recalled, 'Admittedly, Emlyn was on his last legs, or maybe that should be leg because he only had one good one left. In spite of that he was a top-class professional: hard-working, dedicated, good trainer. I always found him fine.' Wolves had finished in the bottom five of the First Division before Hughes arrived at the club, but in his first season at Molineux they ended up in sixth position in the League.

Emlyn Hughes also went on to win further England caps after he left Liverpool. Ron Greenwood selected Hughes for the England squad that participated in the 1980 Home International Championship. He played against Northern Ireland and then made his farewell England appearance when coming on as a substitute against Scotland. Greenwood's team were beating the Scots 2-0 when Hughes was called upon to keep the Scotland danger man Kenny Dalglish quiet for the rest of the game. England held on to their 2-0 lead and Hughes didn't give his former Anfield teammate a sniff of a chance.

Apart from helping Wolves to climb the League table in his first season at the club, Emlyn Hughes also achieved success in the one domestic competition that had so far eluded him. Wolves' triumph in the 1980 Football League Cup final at Wembley against Nottingham Forest meant that the kid from Barrow had now won practically every club honour in the game.

Wolves reached Wembley with wins over Burnley, Crystal Palace, Queens Park Rangers, Grimsby and Swindon. The Molineux club were a team on the up under manager John Barnwell and the only disappointing aspect of an otherwise successful campaign was a 3-0 home defeat against Watford in the FA Cup. The Watford defeat came a few weeks before the League Cup final and they also lost McAlle with a broken leg.

The following week Wolves travelled to Norwich and won 4-0, Emlyn Hughes having an outstanding game. Nottingham Forest received bad news on the eve of the final when key defender and Hughes' former Anfield teammate, Larry Lloyd, received a one-match suspension from the FA that put him out of the game. It would have been Lloyd's third consecutive appearance in the League Cup final, Nottingham Forest having won the trophy for the past two seasons.

On the day of the final all the newspaper talk was of the two £1 million players on view, Trevor Francis of Forest and Andy Gray of Wolves, and also whether Wolves skipper Emlyn Hughes would finally win a Football League Cup winner's medal? Wolves boss John Barnwell had seen his side warm up for the game with a midweek victory over local rivals Aston Villa. Barnwell, however, felt that his team still lacked consistency. 'Every time we hit a peak we suffer a setback soon afterwards,' he said. 'We were the first side to win at Old Trafford this season, but then lost to Watford in the FA Cup. We then had a magnificent victory over Liverpool, but then lost to Middlesbrough. I'm making no predictions for the final.'

The final against Brian Clough's Nottingham Forest was far from a classic. Wolves had Hughes and Berry at the heart of their defence trying to stifle the Forest danger men, Francis and Birtles. Clough's team was packed with outstanding talent, none more so than England goalkeeper Peter Shilton. Wolves' strike force of Andy Gray and John Richards had few chances to trouble Shilton in the opening action of the game. Andy Gray admitted in his book *Gray Matters* that he always liked to try and rough up Shilton in the early stages of a match. 'I'd set the boys to try and hang a ball up in the box, so I could challenge him and give him a real bang,' recalled the powerhouse striker. Whether Shilton had his mind on the next buffeting from Gray is not known, but it was a mistake by the normally reliable Forest goalkeeper that cost them the match. Peter Daniel hit a high ball into the Forest penalty area, but David Needham looked like he had the situation under control as he went to clear the ball. Peter Shilton, however, ran from his line and plunged straight into Needham. In the confusion the ball fell to Andy Gray who had the simple task of placing the ball into the net. It was the only goal of an otherwise uneventful match.

Nottingham Forest put Wolves under severe pressure for the rest of the game and Emlyn Hughes marshalled his defence superbly to enable his side to maintain their one-goal lead. Andy Gray said of Hughes, 'Emlyn was gigantic. We blocked them with everything we had. We hacked the ball clear every time we got it and rode our luck.' The League Cup was the one trophy Emlyn hadn't won and he was determined to give it everything and lead by example. Inspired by an outstanding Emlyn Hughes performance Wolves held on for a famous victory. It was a rare trophy success for Wolverhampton Wanderers, a club that had been one of the best teams in the land in the 1950s, but were now a fading shadow of Stan Cullis' great teams of that decade.

Another special moment for Emlyn Hughes during his stint at
Wolves took place in the weeks before their League Cup victory.
Emlyn was the subject of a *This is Your Life* television programme. The
surprised Wolves skipper was presented with the famous red book
after their home game against Liverpool, which they won 1-0. The
Liverpool team were all in on it and agreed to stay behind after the
game to pay their own tribute to the former Anfield great. Bill Shankly
travelled to the Midlands for the programme, and gave the viewers the
line about being afraid to go back to Blackpool after paying £65,000
for the teenage Hughes in case they locked him up for daylight
robbery!

Emlyn Hughes might now have been plying his trade for Wolves,
but he was still a much loved figure by the supporters back at Anfield.
His reception when he led out Wolves at his former stomping ground
during the 1979/80 season brought tears to the eyes of the clearly
moved Hughes.

Emlyn Hughes' second season at Wolves was not as successful as the
1979/80 campaign and he featured in only half of their League games.
His dodgy knee was once again proving a problem and in the summer
of 1981 he accepted an offer from Second Division Rotherham United
to become their player-manager. Hughes' stint at Wolves had been an
unqualified success and the Molineux crowd just wished that he could
have joined the club earlier in his football career. Wolves manager John
Barnwell had nothing but praise for Hughes. He said, 'The greatest
thing about Emlyn was his enthusiasm. He would make a cup of tea
better than anyone, play snooker better than anyone, his opinion was
always better than yours – that was the character of Emlyn; he hated
being beaten.'

Hughes was also at this stage in his life starting to make a name
for himself as a television and media personality. He had appeared
on several television programmes and was also involved in a major
national road-safety campaign. With his broad smile and confident, lively persona there was no shortage of offers for television
work.

For the time being, however, his main preoccupation was getting
Second Division Rotherham a promotion spot. Rotherham had a

The Wolves boss John Barnwell. Barnwell took Emlyn Hughes to Molineux in 1979 when Liverpool regarded him as surplus to requirements at Anfield. Hughes captained Wolves in their League Cup final success against Nottingham Forest in 1980.

fine season under Emlyn Hughes' management, finishing seventh in Division Two. Rotherham were up with the pace all season for a promotion spot, but a 2-2 draw against Sheffield Wednesday in their penultimate game of the season ended their dreams of First Division football. 'If we had won against Sheffield Wednesday, we would have only needed to win our last game of the season against Wrexham away to go up. Instead we finished seventh,' exclaimed a rueful Emlyn Hughes at the end of his first season as a manager.

Even as a player-manager, Emlyn Hughes' desire to be a winner could sometimes lead to flare-ups with the opposition. During one game against Yorkshire rivals Sheffield Wednesday, Hughes won a penalty in the last minute and Rotherham scored from the penalty kick to take the points. Wednesday boss Jack Charlton, was furious and reckoned that Emlyn had conned the referee. Wednesday player Andy McCulloch described what happened next: 'Jack could be very quick-tempered. I remember Jack and the trainer Tony Toms got Emlyn up against a wall after the game. Tomsy literally had him up in the air while Jack had a real go at him. Emlyn's voice was getting squeakier and squeakier.'

The following season Rotherham failed to show the same sparkle and after the club had a change of ownership Hughes was sacked as manager. After a brief spell as a player again at Hull, Mansfield and Swansea, Emlyn Hughes retired from football in 1983. Hughes talked to sports journalist Charles Lambert for his book *The Boss* in 1995 and told him that being a football manager was not for him. 'The profession has become a merry-go-round,' he said. 'There are only so many managers about – one gets the sack and within a week he's appointed to a new job somewhere else.'

As for football itself, he proclaimed that it didn't hold the same interest for him that it once did: 'The only time I miss the game is when I get together with the ex-players and managers for charity games. Other than that, I never think about it.' Hughes also revealed that he regretted his decision not to take up an offer to take over at a First Division club while managing Rotherham. The club concerned was not named.

CHAPTER 17

'Well done mate, you can come back again' – Emlyn Hughes to Princess Anne when she was a special guest on the 200th edition of *A Question of Sport*.

Emlyn Hughes might have retired from football in 1983, but he was destined to become even more famous nationally for his performances away from the game.

For his services to football Hughes had been awarded the OBE in 1980. Hughes had been brought up back in Barrow as a youngster by his father Fred to be an ardent monarchist. When he was due to receive his OBE he was tipped off that it was to be Prince Philip who would bestow the honour on him. Hughes decided to make an excuse that he couldn't attend on that particular day and was relieved to find that when he did actually turn up at Buckingham Palace on the new date it was the Queen herself who was dishing out the honours. 'All I ever wanted to do was meet her,' he later remarked.

Emlyn Hughes' fondness for the royal family led him to form an unlikely friendship with Princess Anne that was the talk of the nation back in the early 1980s. Hughes actually met the Princess for the first time when Liverpool beat Newcastle in the 1974 FA Cup final at Wembley. Princess Anne handed the jubilant Reds skipper the cup after his team's fine victory. He met her again when he cajoled BBC sports presenter David Coleman into arranging an introduction for him with Princess Anne and her then husband Captain Mark Phillips at the first day of the Aintree Grand National meeting.

Hughes was totally besotted with the royals and his next meeting with Princess Anne on *A Question of Sport* caused something of a sensation.

Emlyn Hughes had appeared on the programme as a guest when it first began and by 1980 he was asked to captain one of the teams on a weekly basis. The opposing captain was England rugby union star Bill Beaumont. The programme was recorded on a Sunday afternoon. The programme that included Princess Anne was the 200th edition of the show. Princess Anne was one of Hughes' team, which also included Scotland rugby union international John Rutherford. Beaumont's team consisted of Olympic sprinter Linford Christie and formula one star Nigel Mansell. Princess Anne was invited on to the programme because of her involvement in the Olympics in the equestrian event.

Back in the early 1980s the royal family was still treated with a great deal of deference by the nation as a whole. Emlyn Hughes' cheeky knockabout performance with the Princess on the programme had two effects. Back on Merseyside, which, in the main, is hardly a strong-hold of monarchism, many thought it was a grovelling performance by the former Liverpool captain. Throughout most of Britain however, the majority of viewers loved Emlyn's treatment of Princess Anne and if he wasn't a television star before the programme was broadcast, he certainly was afterwards. People who had no interest whatsoever in football now knew who Emlyn Hughes was. Some detested Emlyn Hughes for his performance with the Princess, but a great many more loved him for it. In present-day society, it is hard to believe that a former professional footballer having half an hour of knockabout fun with a member of the royal family on a quiz programme would cause much interest at all. Back in the early 1980s it certainly caused a stir.

Emlyn Hughes and his fellow team captain on *A Question of Sport*, Bill Beaumont, first met on *The Terry Wogan Show* on BBC television in the late 1970s. They got on well and Beaumont was invited to appear on Emlyn Hughes' team in *A Question of Sport*. At that time Emlyn was captain of one team and the Wales rugby union star Gareth Edwards was the opposition captain. Beaumont then became a team captain himself, with jockey Willie Carson captain of the other team. Beaumont said he got on okay with Carson but enjoyed the programme more when the horse racing star was replaced by the returning Emlyn Hughes: 'Although we would meet at the BBC Manchester studios for a chat, I wouldn't say we were bosom pals.

Willie wasn't the kind of bloke I would go off and have a drink with, unlike my two subsequent opposing captains Emlyn Hughes and Ian Botham.' Bill Beaumont found Hughes a kindred spirit and recalled in his autobiography their first meeting: 'At the time Emlyn was playing for Wolverhampton Wanderers. Because of his family connections, he knew rugby quite well and was always keen to get to internationals down in Cardiff.'

Apart from television work Emlyn Hughes had dabbled in other business interests and at one time in the late 1970s owned a sports shop with his former Anfield teammate John Toshack. The shop was situated where Hughes lived on the outskirts of Liverpool in Formby. Emlyn Hughes admitted that he found it hard to come down on people who reneged on payments, whereas his business colleague, John Toshack, was far more hardline.

It was estimated that Emlyn Hughes made over £100,000 from his testimonial season, which was granted to Liverpool players who had been at the club for ten years or more. Always a lover of a flutter on the horses since the days when his family would take him to Cartmel races, he invested some of the money in becoming a racehorse owner. He had a share in a horse called Privy Star trained by Peter Easterby and then another horse by the name of La Cilla. La Cilla was the more successful of the two, winning three races.

Emlyn Hughes' infatuation with horse racing had led to him once asking England manager Ron Greenwood if it would be okay for himself, Mick Mills and his Anfield teammate Phil Thompson to hire a helicopter to travel to the 1980 Derby. The amiable Greenwood readily agreed to Emlyn's request.

Another fellow gambler in the England ranks, Stan Bowles, once had a bust-up with Hughes at an England training camp. Bowles and several of the other players wanted to put in a request for an extra £200 each, to be paid on top of their match fee. The fervent patriot Emlyn Hughes, who sang the national anthem with more gusto than any of his fellow England teammates, was horrified. Emlyn told Stan that he would play for his country for nothing and to think of the three lions on his shirt. Stan Bowles shook his head and replied, 'In that case you can have my three lions and I'll have your £200!'

A proud Emlyn Hughes at Buckingham Palace in March 1980 to receive his
OBE from the Queen. Emlyn's wife Barbara and six-year-old daughter Emma
accompanied him to London for the ceremony. From the moment they were born
Emma and her younger brother Emlyn junior were the football star's pride and
joy. Despite his illness, Emlyn Hughes walked Emma down the aisle when she got
married at London's St Paul's Cathedral in 2004.

Former Liverpool manager Bill Shankly launches his new LP in May 1981. Two of Shankly's former players, Denis Law and Emlyn Hughes, attended the launch to help in the promotion of the album of Shankly's thoughts on football. There had never been a football manager before Bill Shankly who knew how to use the media, and photographers in particular, to increase his public profile and that of his club. Shankly knew the value of giving photographers what they wanted, and in return the iconic image that he was keen to present began to take on a life of its own. The Shankly legend continues to grow with each passing year. The photogenic Emlyn Hughes also knew the value of being media friendly, both as a footballer and also in his television career. He undoubtably had a good tutor in Bill Shankly.

Emlyn Hughes' proudest moment as a racehorse owner came in the 1979 Grand National when he was the sole owner of one of the runners, Wayward Scot. Ladbrokes approached Hughes in 1978 and told him that he would gain a lot of publicity during his testimonial year at Anfield if he owned a Grand National runner. The organisers of the Aintree meeting even said that they would name a race after him. Hughes accepted and the horse, trained by Don 'Ginger' McCain, was prepared for the 1979 race. Ginger was of course the trainer of legendary Grand National winner Red Rum. Wayward Scot however was no Red Rum and had little chance of winning the race.

Although Emlyn Hughes was thrilled to have a runner in the world's most famous horse race, he didn't even get to see it run. Liverpool were playing Manchester United in an FA Cup semi-final at Maine Road, Manchester on the day of the 1979 Grand National. Emlyn Hughes obtained the result of the race at half-time in the drawn match. He was relieved to find out that Wayward Scot had finished the race safe and sound, even though he had failed to complete the course. The winner of the race was 25/1 shot Rubstic.

Emlyn did manage to retrieve some of his outlay on Wayward Scot when it won at Uttoxetera few weeks after the Grand National. Hughes' friendship with Ginger McCain lasted until Emlyn's untimely death in 2004.

1 *Right:* Emlyn Hughes tackles his future England teammate Francis Lee during a 1967 game between Liverpool and Manchester City at Anfield.

2 *Below:* Liverpool squad, 1968. From left to right, back row: Bryne, Strong, Clemence, Lawrence, Lawler, Stevenson Hunt. Front row: St John, Callaghan, Arrowsmith, Hateley, Yeats, Hughes, Thompson, Smith.

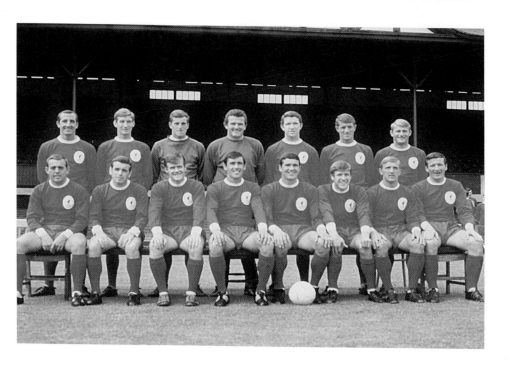

3 The England World Cup squad with manager Alf Ramsey at a training session for the 1970 tournament in Mexico. England's 1966 World Cup hero Roger Hunt travelled to Mexico to watch the England games as a spectator. Emlyn's father Fred also travelled to Mexico but his son was not selected for a single game. Hunt told Emlyn when he next saw him back home in England that Fred never bothered to watch the games, he just sat looking at his son sitting on the bench.

4 Liverpool squad, 1971. From left to right, back row: Thompson, Lindsay, Clemence, Lawrence, Lawler, Ross. Middle row: Evans, McLaughlin, Lloyd, Toshack, Heighway, Boersma, Hall. Front row: Graham, Hughes, Yeats, Shankly (manager), Smith, Callaghan, Paisley (coach).

5 Liverpool's Emlyn Hughes and Brian Hall in action against Arsenal in the 1971 FA Cup final. Charlie George, who scored Arsenal's winner, is the other player in the picture. Hughes apologised to Liverpool boss Bill Shankly after the game, blaming himself for Arsenal's equalising goal. Shankly consoled the young midfielder, telling him that everyone makes mistakes, before walking away muttering, 'There goes the man who lost Liverpool the FA Cup...' Arsenal won 2-1 after extra time.

6 Emlyn Hughes runs out for Liverpool before a 1973 Anfield encounter.

7 Emlyn Hughes and Phil Thompson celebrate in the Liverpool dressing room after winning the League Championship in 1973.

8 The Liverpool team line up with Bill Shankly before the start of the 1974 FA Cup final. Liverpool went on to beat Newcastle 3-0, with Steve Heighway and Kevin Keegan (two) the goalscorers.

9 Emlyn Hughes is introduced to Princess Anne before the start of the 1974 FA Cup final. It was their first meeting and it began a friendship that lasted until Emlyn's death in 2004.

10 Liverpool captain Emlyn Hughes tosses up with Newcastle captain Bobby Moncur before the start of the 1974 FA Cup final.

11 *Above:* The Liverpool squad that Bob Paisley inherited when Bill Shankly retired in 1974. From left to right, back row: Lawler, Boersma, Lloyd, Clemence, Lane, Toshack, Kennedy, Thompson. Front row: Hall, Lindsay, Callaghan, Smith, Shankly (manager), Hughes, Heighway, Cormack, Keegan.

12 *Left:* Emlyn Hughes and former Liverpool boss Bill Shankly parade the FA Charity Shield around Wembley after Liverpool had beaten Leeds in a penalty shootout finale in August 1974. This was the infamous match when Kevin Keegan and Billy Bremner were sent off for fighting.

13 *Opposite above:* Emlyn Hughes seen here in action for England against Scotland at Wembley in May 1973. Scotland's Billy Bremner is also in the picture. England won the game 1-0 through a Martin Peters goal.

14 *Below:* During their 1974 tour of Eastern Europe, England captain Emlyn Hughes exchanges pennants with Yugoslavia captain Dragan Dzajic before the start of a friendly international. The game ended in a 2-2 draw, Mick Channon and Kevin Keegan scoring the goals for England.

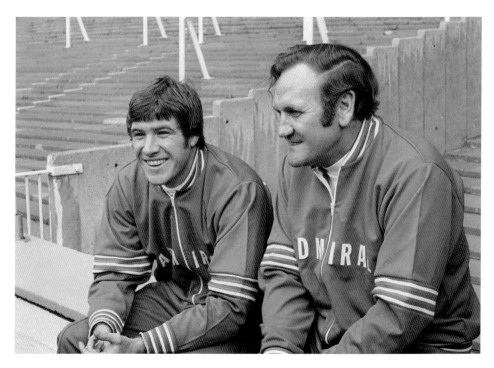

15 *Above:* Emlyn Hughes and Don Revie at an England get-together in October 1974. Revie became manager in July 1974, but Hughes fell out with him after he dropped the Liverpool captain from the England team in March 1975. Hughes was recalled eighteen months later but he and Revie never enjoyed a good relationship.

17 *Above:* Emlyn Hughes in action against Queens Park Rangers during the 1976/77 season.

18 *Right:* Emlyn Hughes with his Footballer of the Year trophy for 1977.

16 *Opposite below:* Emlyn Hughes pictured with, from left to right, Dennis Tueart, Mick Channon, Kevin Keegan and Stan Bowles at an England training camp in May 1976. Hughes was shocked to hear that some of his England teammates had put in a request for an extra £200 for playing in international matches. He told them that he would play for his country for nothing. Stan Bowles stunned the fiercely patriotic Hughes by replying, 'In that case you can have my three lions and I'll have your £200!'

19 *Above:* A jubilant Emlyn Hughes doffs his top hat to the cameras after Liverpool's 1977 European Cup success.

20 *Left:* Emlyn Hughes holds a mini-replica of the European Cup on his head after Liverpool's stunning 3-1 victory over Borussia Moenchengladbach in the 1977 final in Rome.

22 *Opposite below:* Emlyn Hughes in action for England against Scotland in May 1977.

21 *Above:* An ecstatic Liverpool supporter congratulates Emlyn Hughes after Liverpool's 1977 European Cup victory.

23 The England side that took on Argentina in June 1977. From left to right, back row: Neal, Hughes, Watson, Cherry, Wilkins, Clemence. Front row: Pearson, Talbot, Keegan, Channon, Greenhoff. Pearson scored England's goal in a 1-1 draw.

24 Taking a rest from England duty. Emlyn Hughes sits on the ball before the start of the June 1977 international against Brazil. Hughes' England teammates are, from left to right: Brian Greenhoff, Phil Neal, Trevor Francis, Dave Watson. The game ended in a 0-0 draw.

25 Kenny Dalglish is congratulated by Emlyn Hughes after his brilliant goal had won the European Cup for Liverpool against Bruges at Wembley in 1978.

26 Emlyn Hughes celebrates Liverpool's victory over Bruges in the 1978 European Cup final with Terry McDermott.

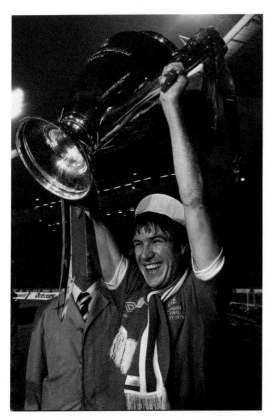

Left: 27 Emlyn Hughes holds the European Cup aloft after Liverpool's 1-0 victory over Bruges in 1978.

Below: 28 Action from the 1978 European Cup first-round tie between Liverpool and Nottingham Forest. Emlyn Hughes fires a shot at the Forest goal. Brian Clough's side beat the Reds over the two legs to send them out of Europe.

Above: 29 Emlyn Hughes is in trouble with the referee during England's game against Northern Ireland at Wembley in June 1980. England drew 1-1 with David Johnson scoring their goal.

Below: 30 Emlyn Hughes in the colours of Wolves, 1981. George Berry is the other Wolves player in the photograph.

31 *Above:* Emlyn Hughes with the Wolverhampton Wanderers squad at the start of the 1980/81 season. From left to right, back row: Villazan, Hibbitt, Brazier, Clarke, Thomas, Richards. Middle row: Palmer, McAlle, Cearns, Bradshaw, Berry, Gray. Front row: Carr, Eves, Daniel, Barnwell (manager), Barker (assistant manager), Hughes, Parkin.

32 *Left:* Emlyn Hughes at Anfield in December 1999. It was forty years since Bill Shankly first joined Liverpool and some of Shankly's boys came together to pay tribute to the great man before the start of the Reds' game against Coventry City.

CHAPTER 18

'Emlyn was a genuine legend, a true great... When I signed for Liverpool he was the main man' – Graeme Souness

Never short of a word or two, Emlyn Hughes supplemented his business interests and television work with regular columns in the sports pages of national newspapers. Some of his comments upset people, like the time he awarded Alex Ferguson the OBE – 'OUT BEFORE EASTER' – during Fergie's early years at Manchester United when they had little success.

Never afraid to speak his mind, Emlyn Hughes also upset his former teammate at Anfield, Alan Hansen, when he wrote in his newspaper column that the Scot's days at Liverpool were numbered. Hughes' comments came after Liverpool's shock defeat against Wimbledon in the 1988 FA Cup final. Recalling Emlyn Hughes' article, Hansen said in his book *A Matter of Opinion* that Emlyn's comments were out of order: 'I feel I had every justification for being angry with Emlyn when he wrote in his column, in May 1988, that my knees had "gone" and that I was finished as a top-class player. He was right about my knees, but I did not retire until 1990.'

Emlyn Hughes also had his say during the period in the 1990s when Graeme Souness was in charge at Anfield. Hughes merely voiced what most Liverpool fans were thinking when he remarked, 'I could weep for what's happening at my old club.'

Emlyn Hughes was being paid however to voice his opinions and nothing was going to stop him from giving them, whether it upset people or not. His views on the modern game always made for interesting reading in his column for *The Mirror* newspaper. When Manchester

Des Lynam, Brendan Foster, Tony Jacklin and Emlyn Hughes photographed here in
1986 to promote the BBC's forthcoming season of sport on television.

United's Eric Cantona was once sent off for violent conduct, Hughes reflected on how the brilliant French star would have fared in his day: 'If Cantona had been playing in my time, there were countless hard men who would have done him without giving away a foul. They would have sat and waited and as soon as he started his tantrums they would have copped him and the referee wouldn't have seen a thing. They would have copped him without even thinking about it and left him lying there. In my day, there were real hard men, the likes of Peter Storey, Terry Paine, Ron Harris, Nobby Stiles, Dave Mackay and the entire Leeds team!'

Emlyn Hughes was still making regular television appearances on *A Question of Sport*, but Bill Beaumont felt by the late 1980s that he and Emlyn were soon to be given the push. Beaumont recalled: 'After three years together we thought we were getting past our sell-by-date. BBC's Northern Head of Sport called us in one day and said he would give us one more series and that would probably be it. We then discovered Emlyn was leaving because he had had an offer to get involved in ITV's equivalent, a programme called *Sporting Triangles*.' Hughes left the BBC to join the ITV programme and initially it received a ratings boost. Former football great Jimmy Greaves was also on *Sporting Triangles* and recalled Emlyn Hughes' impact: 'Emlyn had an immediate impact on the show. His happy-go-lucky demeanour and good general knowledge of sport had a very positive effect. Emlyn Hughes was very good for the show and we had a lot of fun working together.'

Sporting Triangles never achieved the level of success that *A Question of Sport* did and probably wasn't a brilliant career move by Emlyn Hughes. It lasted for a couple more series and was then dropped by ITV.

Throughout the 1990s Emlyn Hughes continued to make television appearances and he was also involved in several other projects. Throughout his football career he was always aware that he had to make the most of his earnings potential, particularly after seeing what happened to some of England's 1966 World Cup heroes. Hughes once said in an interview, 'You look at what that side did. Bobby Moore's the only England player ever to pick up a World Cup and he didn't make two shillings out of doing it. That was the way it was.'

Hughes ran a promotions company based in Yorkshire in the 1990s named VIKTOR. He also hosted a phone-in for Yorkshire-based Real Radio and worked at the station for several years. He still did media work and after-dinner speaking engagements. He also endorsed sports sweaters with their own special logos on.

Although he now lived in Sheffield, he returned to Liverpool on several occasions, most notably in 2002 when he attended a reunion night at the Crown Plaza Hotel for the 1977 European Cup winning team. It was the twenty-fifth anniversary of that historic night and guest of honour was Bob Paisley's widow Jessie. 'You had to be champions back in 1977 to compete in the European Cup. Now you can come fourth, third and second and get into the Champions League,' declared Mrs Paisley. 'It's not the same. The knockout style was much more exciting,' she concluded.

Emlyn Hughes, Liverpool's captain on that historic night back in May 1977 in Rome, remarked, 'We were lucky enough before Bob Paisley to have Bill Shankly, Rueben Bennett, Joe Fagan and Ronnie Moran. We had the great players of the 1960s, who helped us win the European Cup because they set the standards. We were fortunate to play for the greatest club in the history of English football.'

Emlyn Hughes seemed to be in such great spirits and general health at the October 2002 European Cup reunion that it came as a complete shock when it was made public that he had been diagnosed with a brain tumour in August 2003. Emlyn Hughes received radiotherapy and chemotherapy treatment in an effort to beat his illness. It was typical of his fighting spirit that he refused to shut himself away and he raised many thousands of pounds with his fundraising efforts for the hospital that was treating him.

Messages were sent to him by the hundred from Liverpudlians and Evertonians, the blue half of Merseyside acknowledging that Emlyn Hughes was indeed a wonderful footballing talent. Although he had taken the mickey out of them over the years, that was now long forgotten.

Emlyn Hughes' great friend Ginger McCain met up with Emlyn at the 2004 Grand National. Ginger had just won with Amberleigh House and noticed the clearly unwell Emlyn Hughes sitting in the

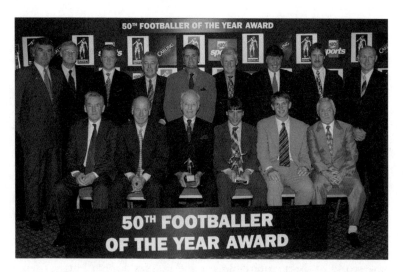

Past and present winners of the Footballer of the Year award at a special ceremony in May 1997. From left to right, back row: Pat Jennings, Bert Slater, Steve Nicol, Ian Callaghan, Frank McLintock, Tony Book, Emlyn Hughes, Frans Thijssen, Clive Allen. Front row: Dave Mackay, Bobby Charlton, Stanley Matthews, Gianfranco Zola, Gary Lineker, Bobby Collins.

press room after the race. Recalling the day in his autobiography, Ginger said, 'He stuck up his thumb and whispered, "Great, Ginge." He was a poorly man, but he had a share in an outsider in the National and he did not want to miss the day. He loved the Grand National like he loved Liverpool Football Club. He was just a lovely, lovely man. I still miss his infectious smile, his enthusiasm and his sportsmanship.'

Despite his worsening condition, Emlyn Hughes walked his daughter Emma up the aisle when she got married at St Paul's Cathedral, London in 2004. Emlyn Hughes idolised his wife and family and he was never happier than when in their company back home in Yorkshire.

A tribute night was held for him in Sheffield a few months before his death and despite the fact that he was now wheelchair-bound, he attended the function. The highlight of the occasion for Emlyn Hughes was when 1966 World Cup hero Roger Hunt walked into the room to spend the evening with his former Liverpool comrade.

Emlyn Hughes lost his long battle with cancer on 9 November 2004. His wife and children were at his bedside at their home in Sheffield. The news saddened the whole of the country, but on Merseyside there was a sense of complete shock. He was just fifty-seven years old. Liverpool City Council leader Mike Storey said, 'Emlyn was one of the city's adopted sons. Even the blue half of the city would recognise that he was passionate about football and committed to the city. He was a very pleasant man – both genuine and warm.' Former Everton great Howard Kendall told the *Liverpool Echo*, 'I lived close to Emlyn in Formby and he would pop in with his little girl Emma on Sunday mornings for a cup of tea – when they had won and we had lost! If it was the other way around you'd never see him. Emlyn was a real character and will be sorely missed.'

Tributes to the former Liverpool star continued to pour in from the world of sport, entertainment and politics. Emlyn Hughes' fame had spread far beyond the world of football. On the day after Emlyn Hughes' death, Liverpool played Middlesbrough in a Carling Cup tie. A minute's silence was impeccably observed by both the Liverpool and Middlesbrough fans who attended the game. Emlyn Hughes' pal at Buckingham Palace, Princess Anne, paid a tribute to the former Kop idol who she described as 'her friend'.

The most moving messages of condolence came from Liverpudlians throughout the world. The *Liverpool Echo* printed brief but poignant messages from as far afield as Dublin, Malta, Ohio, Australia, Japan, America, Vancouver, Sweden and places throughout the globe. All wanted to pay their last respects to 'Crazy Horse', Emlyn Hughes, a player they idolised and who epitomised everything that was great about Liverpool Football Club during their golden years of the 1970s.

EMLYN HUGHES' GOLDEN MOMENTS

Holland 0 England 1
Friendly, Amsterdam, 5 November 1969

Emlyn Hughes made his England debut against Holland in the Olympic Stadium, Amsterdam on 5 November 1969. His tenacious action-packed style of play appealed to England manager Alf Ramsey and the Liverpool player looked a good bet to force his way into the England squad for the 1970 World Cup finals in Mexico.

Hughes had been selected by Ramsey for several England squads and had also represented the Under-23s at international level. The England boss decided to give Hughes his full England chance on Bonfire Night in the Dutch capital playing at left-back. Emlyn Hughes had a solid game alongside Everton's Tommy Wright at right-back and England regulars Jack Charlton and Bobby Moore the other defenders in a 4-4-2 formation.

Holland had the brilliant Johan Cruyff in their line-up, and the Ajax forward put the England defence under severe pressure with several dazzling runs. Emlyn Hughes was grateful that Cruyff was employed by Holland on the left wing and it was left to Tommy Wright to attempt to keep a grip on the home team's star performer.

Although an international debut is a nerve-racking experience for most players, Emlyn Hughes slotted into the England defence well, the brilliant Bobby Moore quietly encouraging and guiding the young full-back throughout the game. Apart from Cruff, Holland's other outstanding performer on a cold wintry evening in Amsterdam was midfielder Rijnders.

England had their own midfield maestro in Bobby Charlton playing in his ninety-sixth international. Emlyn Hughes' Liverpool teammate Peter Thompson also made a brief appearance in this game, coming on for Francis Lee in the closing minutes.

England's defence held firm against the talented Holland forward line; Chelsea's Peter Bonetti, playing in goal in place of Gordon Banks, making several fine saves. A goal from Colin Bell five minutes from the end, when he latched on to a miscued Bobby Charlton effort and blasted the ball past Trejtel, ensured that Emlyn Hughes' England debut was a winning one.

Holland: Trestel, Drost, Israel, Ejkenbrock, Krol, Veenstra (Van Dijk), van Hanegen, Dulder, Rijnders, Cruyff, Rensenbrink.
England: Bonetti, Wright, Hughes, Mullery, J. Charlton, Moore, Lee (Thompson), Bell, R. Charlton, Hurst, Peters.

Liverpool 2 Athletic Bibao 1
Inter-Cities Fairs Cup first round, Anfield, 2 October 1968
Emlyn Hughes scored his first goal in a European competition for Liverpool when they played Spanish Club Athletic Bibao in the Inter Cities Fairs Cup on 2 October 1968. Liverpool had lost the away leg in Spain 2-1. Nearly 50,000 fans attended the return game at Anfield hopeful that Bill Shankly's team would overturn the one-goal deficit. It was Bilbao, however, who opened the scoring when Uriarte passed to Aroitia who displayed great skill to sidestep Tommy Smith's lunging tackle and beat Tony Lawrence after taking the ball past the Liverpool goalkeeper.

Anfield was stunned. The home team had done most of the attacking, but the Spaniards looked a distinctly useful outfit as they warded off the Reds' attacks and then hit Liverpool on the break. The goal came after thirty-two minutes and Liverpool went in at the break looking as though they had little chance of pulling back Bilbao's two-goal cushion.

Bill Shankly geed up his boys for an all out effort in the second half and Liverpool laid siege to the Bilbao goal after the interval. The breakthrough came when, twelve minutes from the end, Ian St John sent in a free-kick for Ron Yeats to head on to Chris Lawler, who nodded the ball past Iribar.

The Kop went wild as Liverpool kept up their all-out assault on the Athletic Bibao goal. Emlyn Hughes, who had been enjoying an outstanding game with his probing runs from midfield, smashed home a close-range effort three minutes from time to make the tie level.

Extra time failed to provide a winner. Alun Evans did have a chance to put the Reds through, but he failed to find the target with only Iribar in the Bilbao goal to beat.

After a magnificent European night at Anfield, Liverpool exited the competition when the game was decided on the toss of a coin, the Liverpool skipper Ron Yeats making the wrong call. When the result was announced Anfield fell into a stunned silence.

Liverpool: Lawrence, Lawler, Wall, Smith, Yeats, Hughes, Callaghan, Hunt, Evans, St John, Thompson.
Athletic Bibao: Iribar, Saez, Aranguren, Aguirre, Echeberria, Larrauri, Zorriqueta, Argoitia, Aricta, Uriate, Rojo.

AEK Athens 1 Liverpool 3
UEFA Cup second round, Athens, 7 May 1972

Emlyn Hughes scored twice for the Reds in this impressive victory away to AEK Athens in November 1972. Liverpool held a 3-0 lead from the first leg of this UEFA Cup tie and although the Greeks put the Reds under severe pressure early on, in the end Liverpool ran out comfortable winners.

Hughes had an outstanding game for Liverpool in the Philadelphia Stadium. With AEK pressing for an early goal, Emlyn Hughes saved his team from going a goal behind when he headed off the line with just a few minutes played. Hughes then silenced the volatile Athens crowd when, after seventeen minutes, he received a free-kick from Tommy Smith and lashed the ball into the net from a full twenty-five yards out. The ball hit the inside of the post before resting in the net. Emlyn Hughes scored some spectacular goals in his Anfield career, but this was one of the best.

AEK kept pressing forward and their industrious play paid off when Hughes was forced into giving away a penalty after handling the ball. Nicoladis scored from the penalty kick to give the Greeks hope. Emlyn Hughes just couldn't be kept out of the game and he began a run at the AEK defence from the half-way line. His momentum carried him through to the edge of the AEK penalty area, where, after receiving a quick return pass from Keegan, he blasted the ball in for Liverpool's second. From that moment on Liverpool controlled the game and it was no surprise when Phil Boersma, who had come on as a substitute for Heighway in the second half, wrapped the game up for the Reds three minutes from the end.

Emlyn Hughes had undoubtedly been the star of the show on a sunny afternoon in Athens.

AEK Athens: Errea, Leslis, Lavaridis, Toskas, Theodoridis, Pianis, Dandelis, Nicolau (Fesaos), Nicoladis, Papalornon, Pouonis (Psimogiannos).
Liverpool: Clemence, Lawler, Lindsay, Smith, Lloyd, Hughes, Keegan, Cormack, Heighway (Boersma), Toshack, Callaghan.

Wales 0 England 3
Home International Championship, Cardiff, 20 May 1972
Emlyn Hughes' one and only goal at full international level came in this 1972 encounter at Cardiff's Ninian Park. Alf Ramsey's team had been drawn to play in a group that comprised themselves, Poland and Wales for a place in the 1974 World Cup finals, so victory over the Welsh was of particular importance as a confidence booster for the more important fixtures that lay ahead over the coming months.

Wales could boast quite a formidable attacking line-up during this period in their history, with Wyn Davies, Ron Davies and John Toshack forming a three-man aerial assault force. The two Davieses were on their day quite brilliant headers of the ball and Emlyn Hughes knew only too well of his Liverpool teammate John Toshack's prowess in the air. England's defence, however, had the commanding Derby centre-back Roy McFarland in their line-up, along with Bobby Moore, Paul Madeley and Hughes. All were quite outstanding and gave the Welsh attack few opportunities. Bobby Moore in particular gave a stirring performance and managed to disguise from the Welsh team the fact that he was playing with a sprained back after injuring himself in the opening minutes.

Emlyn Hughes' goal came after twenty-five minutes when he latched on to the ball after Gary Sprake in the Wales goal failed to hold a shot from Colin Bell and Hughes drove the ball into the net. Overall, Hughes was probably England's outstanding player on the day with his non-stop running from full-back. His overlapping runs caused the Welsh defence problems throughout the game and Hughes had one of his finest games in the England shirt.

Rodney Marsh scored England's second goal with a fierce strike from fifteen yards out. Manchester City's Mike Summerbee, marauding up the right wing, crossed for his City teammate Colin Bell to score number three and wrap up a convincing England victory.

Wales had started the game with high hopes that they would defeat the English for the first time since 1955, but Ramsey's boys had other ideas.

Wales: Sprake, Rodriguez, England, Roberts (Reece), Thomas, Durban, Hennessey, Yorath, R. Davies, W. Davies, Toshack.
England: Banks, Madeley, McFarland, Moore, Hughes, Storey, Bell, Hunter, Summerbee, MacDonald, Marsh.

Liverpool 2 Eintracht Frankfurt 0
UEFA Cup first round, first leg, Anfield, 12 September 1972
Emlyn Hughes scored Liverpool's second goal in this 2-0 victory over Eintract Frankfurt in the UEFA Cup at Anfield in September 1972. Liverpool went on to win the competition the following May, their first success in Europe in the club's history.

This first-round tie was not expected to be an easy game for the Reds. German opposition was always tough. Kevin Keegan looked to be yards offside when Hughes found him with a through ball. Playing to the whistle, Keegan popped the ball into the net and, despite the justified protests from the Eintract players, the referee allowed the goal to stand. This early breakthrough was expected to bring the German side out of their defensive mode, but they still continued to play a containing game, making just a few forays into the Liverpool half.

In the second half Liverpool went in search of the vital second goal that would make the return leg in Germany in two weeks time an easier task. Despite several near misses, the Reds failed to get a second until fifteen minutes from the end. It was Emlyn Hughes who came to

Liverpool's rescue, when he strode into the Germans' penalty area to get on to the end of a Peter Cormack centre to put the Reds 2-0 up. In the final minutes of the game it was one-way traffic as Shankly's team pushed forward for more goals. Despite several near misses, Eintracht kept the score down to 2-0 for the return leg.

For the game in Germany two weeks later Trevor Storton, signed from Liverpool's Merseyside neighbours Tranmere Rovers, came on as a substitute for the injured Tommy Smith. Liverpool held on for a 0-0 draw, mainly due to a brilliant display from their goalkeeper, Ray Clemence.

Liverpool: Clemence, Lawler, Lindsay, Smith, Lloyd, Hughes, Keegan, Cormack, Heighway, Toshack, Callaghan.
Eintracht Frankfurt: Kunter, Kolb, Lutz, Kliemann, Rohrbach, Grabowski, Parits, Nickel, Comca, Heese, Wiedle.

Scotland 0 England 5
Friendly, Hampden Park, 14 February 1973
This was the great Bobby Moore's 100th appearance for his country and what better way to celebrate it than to thrash the old enemy Scotland 5-0 in their own back yard? Emlyn Hughes was winning his twenty-first cap in a game that was one of the highlights of his international career. Scotland were in the process of beginning their centenary celebrations, but Ramsey's boys definitely spoilt the party.

England took the lead after only six minutes when Clarke's centre hit Channon and was then diverted into his own net by Peter Lorimer. Emlyn Hughes then got in on the action when he hit a long pass through the centre of the Scotland defence for Channon to out-jump Colquhoun and head to Clarke who hit goal number two.

The home team were shell-shocked and just one minute later Channon received a long throw from Chivers and lashed the ball past the Scotland goalkeeper for number three. Only a quarter of an hour had gone and England were already three goals to the good. England had only scored 13 goals in their previous 11 games, but on this bitterly cold evening in Glasgow on a pitch that had a dusting of snow on it, their attack was on fire.

Scotland could boast some outstanding talent in their line-up, such as Dalglish, Bremner, Buchan, Lorimer and Macari, but they looked totally outclassed. With Bobby Moore and Emlyn Hughes superb in defence and Peters, Bell and Ball dominating the midfield, it looked like Alf Ramsey was building a team that could challenge for the 1974 World Cup.

As it turned out, Poland's shock victory over England in a World Cup qualifier just a few months later, followed by their return draw in the game at Wembley, eliminated England and cost Alf his job. The Polish disaster was, however, a long way from England's thoughts on a memorable evening in Glasgow in February 1973. Further goals from Chivers and Clarke gave England a 5-0 victory over the Scots, matching their best ever victory over Scotland in Glasgow, achieved in 1888. It was one of the great days of Emlyn Hughes' international career.

No doubt Emlyn Hughes couldn't wait to get back to Anfield to give Bill Shankly a blow-by-blow account of how his fellow countrymen were put to the sword by England.

Scotland: Clark, Forsyth, Donachie, Bremner, Colquhoun, Buchan, Lorimer, Dalglish, Macari, Graham, Morgan.
England: Shilton, Storey, Hughes, Bell, Madeley, Moore, Ball, Channon, Chivers, Clarke, Peters.

Everton 0 Liverpool 2
Football League First Division, Goodison Park, 3 March 1973
In front of a 54,000 attendance at Goodison Park, Liverpool won this March 1973 derby against Everton 2-0. Emlyn Hughes scored both of Liverpool's goals as they romped to a convincing victory. Liverpool had only won two of their League games at the start of 1973 and victory over Everton was vital if they were to get their attempt to win their first League title since 1966 back on track.

Emlyn Hughes' first goal came after eighty minutes when Ian Callaghan played a brilliant through ball to the marauding midfielder Hughes, who knocked the ball wide of the Everton goalkeeper David Lawson before striking it into an empty net.

The Liverpudlians inside Goodison erupted as their song about 'The Mighty Emlyn' rang around the stadium. When Hughes scored his second with just two minutes remaining, his name was chanted even louder by the Liverpool fans. The second came when Alec Lindsay hit a long ball into the Everton penalty area. Lawson, the Everton goal-keeper, could only manage to punch the ball out, but unfortunately for his team it went straight to Hughes, who volleyed it with enormous power straight into the net.

Emlyn Hughes was already a player whom the Liverpool fans idol-ised. At that moment in time their devotion went up a few more notches. To the Anfield brethren, Emlyn Hughes was the pride of Merseyside that Saturday evening and for many more years to come.

Everton: Lawson, Wright, Styles, Hurst, Kenyon, Darracott, Jones, Kendall, Harper, Lyons, Connolly.
Liverpool: Clemence, Lawler, Lindsay, Smith, Lloyd, Hughes, Keegan, Hall, Boersma, Heighway, Callaghan.

Liverpool 1 Tottenham Hotspur 0
UEFA Cup semi-final first leg, Anfield, 10 April 1973
Liverpool laid siege to the Spurs goal for almost the entire ninety min-utes of this 1973 UEFA Cup semi-final first leg, but had only a one-goal lead to take back to White Hart Lane for the return encounter.

Bob Paisley had warned his team to expect a fierce test against their London opponents and Pat Jennings and his Spurs colleagues fought like tigers from the kick-off. Spurs had actually drawn their last six games against Liverpool at Anfield, so the form book pointed to a tight encounter. On his last visit to Anfield, Jennings had saved two spot-kicks, so Liverpool knew that even if they breached the Spurs defence, the Irish goalkeeper would still take some beating.

Through a mixture of good luck and Liverpool's over-anxious approach to gaining an early breakthrough, Spurs kept the home team at bay for almost half an hour before Alec Lindsay made the breakthrough. The goal came when Tommy Smith floated a free kick into the Spurs penalty area. The away team failed to clear the ball and Lindsay pounced to score the only goal of the game.

Smith almost added a second when a superbly struck free-kick was brilliantly saved by Jennings diving full length to push the shot around the post. Steve Heighway then blasted the ball against the bar as Liverpool peppered the Spurs goal with shot after shot.

Liverpool thought that the all-important second goal had come when Mike England pulled down Kevin Keegan in the penalty area, but the referee waved play on. The only Liverpool player not to get in a strike at the Spurs goal was goalkeeper Ray Clemence, who had a relatively carefree evening watching his team launch wave after wave of attacks at the away team's goal.

Spurs held on for a creditable 1-0 defeat but despite the fact that they beat the Reds 2-1 in the second leg, they were eliminated on the away goals rule.

Liverpool: Clemence, Lawler, Lindsay, Smith, Lloyd, Hughes, Keegan, Cormack, Hall, Heighway (Boersma), Callaghan.
Tottenham Hotspur: Jennings, Kinnear, Knowles, Coates (Pearce), England, Beal, Gilzean, Perryman, Chivers (Evans), Peters, Pratt.

Liverpool 2 Leeds United 0
Football League First Division, Anfield, 23 April 1973

The excellent 2-0 victory against Leeds at Anfield in April 1973 more or less wrapped up Emlyn Hughes' first League title success at Liverpool. Shankly's boys needed just one more point from their final game of the season at home to Leicester City to be mathematically certain of winning the championship. Liverpool's closest pursuers, Arsenal, had a tough away trip to Southampton to contend with, so if the Reds could take the points against Leeds it looked certain that Bill Shankly would achieve his third championship success at Anfield.

A crowd of just under 56,000 packed into Anfield and from the outset it was clear that the Reds would have to fight hard to take the points. Don Revie's team were out of the title race, but they still had an FA Cup final against Sunderland to look forward to. They were also in the semi-finals of the European Cup-Winners' Cup. Key Leeds players Johnny Giles and Mick Jones were missing for this game, but the side was still packed with talent.

It was Peter Cormack who put Liverpool's nerves at ease when he opened the scoring just after the start of the second half. Cormack's goal was set up by Lloyd and Lawler, who exchanged headed passes from a Hall corner before Cormack beat David Harvey with a low drive. Allan Clarke almost equalised for Leeds, blasting over the bar from close range. Kevin Keegan, having an outstanding game, wrapped up the victory five minutes from the end when Harvey dived to cut out a Cormack cross, but Keegan was on hand to hit the ball into the roof of the net.

Anfield erupted in a scene of joyous celebration. News then filtered through that Arsenal had dropped a point at Southampton. The League Championship was back on Merseyside.

Liverpool: Clemence, Lawler, Hughes, Smith, Lloyd, Thompson, Keegan, Cormack, Hall, Heighway, Callaghan.
Leeds United: Harvey, Reaney, Cherry, Bremner, Ellam, Hunter, Lorimer, Clarke, Jordan, Yorath, Madeley.

Liverpool 3 Borussia Moenchengladbach 0
UEFA Cup final first leg, Anfield, 10 May 1973

Liverpool took a giant step to winning their first European trophy with this emphatic victory over Borussia Moenchengladbach in the first leg of the 1973 UEFA Cup final.

After torrential rain caused the abandonment of the original fixture on 9 May, the two teams returned to Anfield the following evening to try again. This time the weather had improved and Liverpool made the most of the better conditions to set up a three-goal lead for the return leg.

Liverpool already had the 1972/73 League title in the bag and Shankly's team were determined to complete a famous trophy-winning double. Kevin Keegan was the star of the show with two goals, but the whole team played at the top of their form. Keegan's first came after twenty-one minutes when Toshack nodded a Lawler cross into his path and the all-action Liverpool forward dived to head the ball past Kleff in the Borussia goal.

In the thirty-third minute Toshack was once again under pressure when he took a pass from Keegan and then laid it back to his strike partner. Keegan drove the ball into the net from close range to put the Reds two up. This should have been his hat-trick because just eight minutes before, Keegan had failed to put away a penalty kick after Bonhof had handled a Lindsay centre.

Liverpool centre half Larry Lloyd wrapped up the game for his team after sixty-one minutes when he rose above the Borussia defence to head home a Keegan corner kick. Liverpool were on fire throughout this encounter and could easily have doubled their goals tally. Borussia did have chances of their own and the Reds had Ray Clemence to thank for keeping the Germans out when he saved brilliantly from a Heynckes penalty kick with twenty-five minutes still to play.

Borussia Monchengladbach did make Liverpool fight all the way for their first European trophy in the return leg two weeks later. They beat the Reds 2-0, but Emlyn Hughes and his Liverpool teammates had just about done enough in the first game to warrant the UEFA Cup.

Liverpool: Clemence, Lawler, Lindsay, Smith, Lloyd, Hughes, Keegan, Cormack, Toshack, Heighway (Hall), Callaghan.
Borussia Moenchengladbach: Kleff, Danner, Michalich, Vogts, Bonhof, Kolik, Jensen, Wimmer, Rupp (Simmonsen), Netzer, Heynckes.

England 7 Austria 0
Friendly, Wembley, 26 September 1973
England warmed up for their crucial 1973 World Cup qualifier against Poland with this stunning 7-0 victory over Austria at Wembley. Alf Ramsey picked the line-up that would face Poland three weeks later, Emlyn Hughes being joined in defence by Paul Madeley, Roy McFarland and Norman Hunter. Austria at the time were hardly a poor team and prior to their game against England had achieved creditable draws against Brazil and Hungary.

Mick Channon scored England's first after ten minutes and Allan Clarke scored the second with a brilliant piece of skill. He controlled a centre from Currie, sold a dummy to Sara and then lashed the ball home. Clarke scored goal number three just before half-time when he shot past the Austrian goalkeeper after receiving a Colin Bell cross.

England carried on with their demolition of Austria in the second half. Mick Channon hit number four when he scored from close range after Clarke's goalbound effort struck a post. With sixty minutes on the clock, Martin Chivers grabbed a slice of the goal feast when he placed a Currie centre past Koncilia for England's fifth.

Emlyn Hughes and his defensive colleagues had had a relatively quiet evening, with Peter Shilton in goal not having to make a save. England were rampant and goal number six came from Tony Currie who had one of the greatest games in an England shirt. Currie's goal came when he volleyed home a beauty into the top corner after latching on to a lob from Mick Channon.

The rout of Austria ended three minutes from time when Colin Bell ended a move involving Currie, Clarke and Channon by hitting his shot hard and low into the bottom corner.

The 7-0 victory was the most spectacular scoreline in Emlyn Hughes' England career.

England: Shilton, Madeley, Hughes, Bell, McFarland, Hunter, Channon, Currie, Chivers, Clarke, Peters.
Austria: Koncilia, Sara, Krieger, Shmidradner, Eigenstiller (Kriess), Hattenberger (Gombasch), Starek, Ettmayer, Kreuz, Krankl, Jara.

Liverpool 3 Newcastle United 0
FA Cup final, Wembley, 4 May 1974
Emlyn Hughes collected his first silverware as Liverpool captain after this emphatic 3-0 victory over Newcastle United in the 1974 FA Cup final.

Bill Shankly had been threatening to produce a great side for a number of seasons at Anfield. In the previous campaign they had collected the First Division title and the UEFA Cup and this magnificent performance was the icing on the cake before Shankly's unexpected retirement.

Before the match soccer pundits had predicted a bold showing from an up-and-coming Newcastle team. With players of the calibre of Alan Kennedy, Terry McDermott, Bobby Moncur, Terry Hibbitt and Malcolm Macdonald in their line-up, Newcastle were quietly fancied to bring some domestic silverware to St James' Park for the first time since the club's glory days of the 1950s.

Despite all the pre-match hype, the truth was that Newcastle were simply outclassed. Liverpool were on a different planet to Newcastle and if they had doubled their 3-0 scoreline it would have still not done justice to the demolition job that they carried out on Malcolm Macdonald and his teammates.

Kevin Keegan opened the scoring for Liverpool after fifty-eight minutes when he sensationally volleyed home a Tommy Smith centre. Steve Heighway scored Liverpool's second in the seventy-fifth minute after Toshack headed the ball on to him. Heighway showed superb control before placing the ball past McFaul in the Newcastle goal. Man of the Match Kevin Keegan scored Liverpool's third two minutes from time when he again latched on to a Smith cross to blast the ball past McFaul.

Liverpool's display in the second half was one of the greatest forty-five minutes of football ever seen in Wembley's long history. When Emlyn Hughes stepped up to lift the trophy it is doubtful that Wembley had ever witnessed a broader grin on a winning captain's face than Emlyn's that May afternoon in 1974.

Liverpool: Clemence, Smith, Lindsay, Thompson, Cormack, Hughes, Keegan, Hall, Heighway, Toshack, Callaghan.
Newcastle: McFaul, Clark, Kennedy, McDermott, Howard, Moncur, Cassidy, Smith (Gibb), Macdonald, Tudor, Hibbitt.

Wales 0 England 2
Home International Championship, Cardiff, 11 May 1974
Emlyn Hughes fulfilled Bill Shankly's prophecy when he signed the Blackpool youngster seven years earlier in this game. The great Shankly predicted that Hughes would go on to become England captain. This Home International Championship encounter against Wales saw Hughes leading out his country for the first time.

After Bobby Moore's international career had come to an end, his West Ham teammate Martin Peters had captained his country several times. Emlyn Hughes was then handed the job by temporary England boss Joe Mercer. It was a dream come true for Hughes to lead England out against the country that his father had appeared for as a rugby league international.

Hughes was selected by Mercer to play in a midfield role on the right and the new England skipper had a solid game, snuffing out the dangerous Welsh forwards Ron Davies and Leighton James. James was hardly given a kick by the combination of Hughes and right-back David Nish. The talented forward was given so few opportunities to display his dribbling skills that he was forced to switch to the right wing in the second half.

After a quiet opening England sprang into life ten minutes before the interval when Stan Bowles scored the first goal. The goal was set up by Todd, Weller and Channon. Channon hit a low cross into the Wales penalty area. Phillips, the Wales goalkeeper could only palm the ball away and Bowles netted with a simple chance.

After the break, England took firm control of the game and their victory was wrapped up by a goal from Kevin Keegan. Weller, Bowles and Nish were involved in the build up. Nish then hit a cross that the Welsh defence failed to clear. Keegan got a touch to the ball and Villars, attempting to clear the ball on his own goal-line, totally missed his kick and the ball trickled into the net.

Emlyn Hughes' career as England captain had got off to a solid start.

Wales: Phillips, Roberts (Cartwright), Roberts, Roberts, Thomas, Yorath, Mahoney, Villars, Reece, Davies (Smallman), James.
England: Shilton, Nish, McFarland, Todd, Pejic, Bell, Hughes, Weller, Keegan, Channon, Bowles.

Liverpool 11 Stromsgodset Drammen 0
European Cup-Winners' Cup first round, Anfield, 17 September 1974

Liverpool's record victory in European competition was this 11-0 thrashing of Norwegian amateurs Stromsgodset Drammen in the European Cup Winners' Cup first-round tie in September 1974. The Reds had put ten past Dundalk in a 1969 Fairs Cup tie at Anfield, but this annihilation of Stromsgodset, apart from being Liverpool's record score in Europe, was also a club record for any competition.

It was obvious from the first few minutes of play that the Norwegians were hopelessly out of their depth as Liverpool went on the rampage. Nine different players registered goals for Liverpool during this game, a feat highly unlikely ever to be bettered. Captain Emlyn Hughes scored the Reds' sixth in the seventy-sixth minute as the Stromsgodset team, a mixture of electricians, printers and car salesmen, found it impossible to get a grip on the skill and extra pace of Bob Paisley's team.

The Norwegians had actually held Don Revie's Leeds United to a draw in a European game the previous season. Emlyn Hughes and his team must therefore have been slightly surprised by how easily Stromsgodset succumbed to the slightest hint of pressure.

Alec Lindsay opened the scoring for Liverpool from the penalty spot after just two minutes. Boersma with two, Peter Thompson with another two, Heighway, Cormack, Smith, Ray Kennedy, Callaghan and Hughes scored the other ten goals. It was Liverpool's biggest victory in their eighty-two-year history. Stromsgodset did have their chances to register a goal themselves, but their nerves got the better of them when they found themselves in goalscoring positions.

Stromsgodset made some amends for their Anfield humiliation in the return leg two weeks later. They held Liverpool to just one goal, a Ray Kennedy effort in a 1-0 victory for the Reds.

Liverpool: Clemence, Smith, Lindsay, Thompson, Cormack, Hughes, Boersma, Hall, Heighway, Kennedy, Callaghan.
Stromsgodset: Thuns, Wolmer, Karlsen, Nostdahl, Pedersen, Amundsen (Withen), Olsen, Henriksen, Halvorsen, Pettersen, T. Olsen (I. Olsen).

Barcelona 0 Liverpool 1
UEFA Cup semi-final, Nou Camp, 30 March 1976
This was one of Liverpool's finest performances in Europe as they fought their way to a magnificent away win over Barcelona. The March 1976 encounter was the first leg of the semi-final of the UEFA Cup. In front of 70,000 fanatical Barcelona fans, Emlyn Hughes skippered

his team to what turned out, in the end, to be quite a comfortable victory.

John Toshack scored the vital early goal in the thirteenth minute when he latched on to a Keegan flick to shoot past Mora in the Barcelona goal. The Nou Camp crowd fell silent and then jeers rang out as Barcelona's attempt to equalise was easily warded off by Hughes and his fellow Liverpool defenders. Barcelona had the Dutch superstars Cruyff and Neeskins in their line-up, but it was Ray Kennedy and Ian Callaghan who controlled the midfield. Phil Thompson, playing alongside Emlyn Hughes at the heart of the Liverpool defence, had an outstanding game.

The truth, however, was that Barcelona barely troubled Ray Clemence in the Liverpool goal, who had only two saves to make all evening. It was Kevin Keegan who looked the major attacking talent on view and but for outstanding saves from Mora he could have bagged a hat-trick. In the final quarter of the game, Barcelona were reduced to hitting long balls into the Liverpool penalty area in a desperate attempt to draw level. Clemence was rarely troubled apart from having to dodge the hundreds of cushions flung onto the pitch by disgruntled Barcelona supporters.

Toshack and Smith went close to doubling Liverpool's lead near the end as a chant of 'Weisweiler out' rang around the stadium. Barcelona's West German manager Hennes Weisweiler knew that if his job rested on his side scoring the two goals needed for them to progress to the final when they travelled to Anfield in two weeks time, then he might as well start packing his bags that evening.

The return leg ended in a 0-0 draw and Liverpool were through to the 1976 UEFA Cup final.

Barcelona: Mora, Miguel, Tome, Marcial, Coraminas, Neeskens, Asenal, Rexach, Mir, Cruyff, Fortes.
Liverpool: Clemence, Smith, Thompson, Hughes, Neal, Callaghan, Kennedy, Case, Heighway, Toshack, Keegan.

Liverpool 3 Bruges 2
UEFA Cup final first leg, Anfield, 28 April 1976

Emlyn Hughes' first taste of European glory as club captain came in this two-legged final of the UEFA Cup in 1976.

The first leg at Anfield was a classic, with the Belgians finding themselves two goals in front after only twelve minutes. Bruges' first goal came when Phil Neal failed to find Clemence with a headed back pass and Lambert nipped in to fire his team ahead after just five minutes. Worse was soon to follow when Cools lashed a shot past Clemence seven minutes later. Liverpool's UEFA Cup hopes looked to be hanging by a thread. When Emlyn Hughes led his team off at half-time the Reds were still two goals behind. Paisley's team, however, were renowned for their fighting spirit and they came storming back in the second half.

Bob Paisley brought on Jimmy Case for John Toshack and pushed Kevin Keegan into a striking role. The switch paid off in dramatic fashion. Steve Heighway found Ray Kennedy twenty yards from the goal and the powerhouse midfielder struck a super shot past Jensen to give Liverpool hope. Kennedy then hit a post with another well-aimed shot and the rebound fell to Case, who put Liverpool level.

The Reds were now rampant and, roared on by the 50,000 crowd packed into Anfield, Steve Heighway dribbled past several Bruges defenders before being brought down in the penalty area. Kevin Keegan stepped up to put Liverpool into a 3-2 lead. In the space of just five minutes Liverpool had turned the game on its head.

Chances were spurned to make the return leg more comfortable for Liverpool, but after being two goals down so early in the game the Reds were overjoyed to be travelling to Belgium with any kind of lead.

The return leg was just as close with Lambert scoring early on for Bruges, only for Keegan to put Liverpool level just three minutes later. The Reds held on for a 1-1 draw and a jubilant Emlyn Hughes proudly collected his first European silverware as Liverpool captain.

Liverpool: Clemence, Neal, Smith, Thompson, Kennedy, Hughes, Keegan, Fairclough, Heighway, Toshack (Case), Callaghan.
Bruges: Jensen, Bastljns, Krieger, Leekens, Volders, Cools, van der Eychen, van Gool, Lambert, de Cubber, le Fevre.

Wolverhampton Wanderers 1 Liverpool 3
Football League First Division, Molineux, 4 March 1976

Emlyn Hughes captained Liverpool to the 1975/76 League Championship, which was clinched with this 3-1 victory over Wolves in May 1976. Wolves needed a victory if they were to have any chance of avoiding relegation. The gates at Molineux were closed well before kick-off with 51,000 inside the ground.

Liverpool were expected to overwhelm the Midlands side from the start. They had been criticised by some for their negative tactics on their travels, and they wanted to take the title playing with some panache. It was Wolves, however, who made the early breakthrough. Steve Kindon scored the opener after thirteen minutes after he ran onto a pass from Richards and crashed the ball past the advancing Clemence. Liverpool were stunned as Molineux erupted. Perhaps there was a chance of Wolves avoiding the dreaded drop to the Second Division after all.

Wolves held out until half-time, mainly through fine saves by Pierce from Ray Kennedy on two occasions. In the second half it was a story of dogged defending by Wolves as Liverpool poured forward in search of an equaliser. Wolves held out until the seventy-sixth minute when Kevin Keegan finally made the breakthrough. Tommy Smith centered for Toshack to find Keegan with a back header; Keegan confidently placed the ball past Pierce to make it 1-1. Nine minutes later, John Toshack put Liverpool in the lead, followed by the clincher a minute before the end from Kennedy.

Liverpool had won the First Division title by one point from Queens Park Rangers. It was heartbreak for the London club hoping to win the first championship in their history. For Wolves it was also a sad night with their relegation to the Second Division confirmed.

For Emlyn Hughes and his team the celebrations went on long into the night. Liverpool boss Bob Paisley was overjoyed to have won his first championship as manager, but he still found time to express sadness at the demise of the once great Wolverhampton Wanderers.

Wolverhampton Wanderers: Pierce, Sunderland, Palmer, Daley, Bailey, Parkin, Carr, Hibbitt, Kindon, Richards, Kelly (Gould).

Liverpool: Clemence, Smith, Neal, Thompson, Kennedy, Hughes, Keegan, Case (Fairclough), Heighway, Toshack, Callaghan.

Crusaders 0 Liverpool 5
European Cup first round, Seaview, 28 September 1976
Liverpool's historic campaign that resulted in their first European Cup triumph in 1977 began against the Northern Ireland Champions, Crusaders, in September 1976. After notching up a comfortable 2-0 home victory against the team from Ulster at Anfield in the first leg, Liverpool travelled to Northern Ireland two weeks later.

Emlyn Hughes and company were confident that the Irish part-timers would provide few problems. A goal from Kevin Keegan after thirty-four minutes made the tie safe for Liverpool, but, unbelievably, Crusaders should have been two up before the England star struck. Crusaders striker McAteer hit the Liverpool woodwork twice before Keegan scored from a David Johnson pass.

In the second half Crusaders held Liverpool to just a one goal lead before the Reds stepped up a gear in the final ten minutes. Liverpool then hit four quick goals to give the scoreline a somewhat flattering look for the Reds. Two goals from Johnson and one each for Heighway and McDermott gave Liverpool a 5-0 victory. It equalled their highest ever away victory in Europe, which was their 5-0 win against the champions of Iceland, Reykjavik, in their first match in Europe in 1964.

Liverpool: Clemence, Neal, Jones, Smith, Kennedy, Hughes, Keegan, Johnson, Heighway, Case (McDermott), Callaghan.
Crusaders: McDonald, Strain, Gorman, McFarland, Gillespie, McPolin, Lennox, McAteer, Kirk, Cooke, McCann.

Liverpool 3 Saint Etienne 1
European Cup quarter-final, Anfield, 16 March 1977
One of the greatest nights in Anfield history saw Emlyn Hughes captain his side to an outstanding victory over the French champions. Trailing 1-0 from the first leg, Liverpool knew they would have to be at their best to progress to the European Cup

semi-finals. The atmosphere inside Anfield was at fever pitch with many thousands locked out as the 'ground full' signs went up well before kick-off.

After just two minutes' play Kevin Keegan sent the home fans delirious when he received a short corner from Heighway and sent in an intended cross that deceived the Saint Etienne goalkeeper and dropped over the line for a fortuitous opener. Saint Etienne hit back in the second half when Bathenay beat Ray Clemence with a stunning strike from twenty-five yards out.

Roared on by their fans, Liverpool fought back immediately when Ray Kennedy sent in a low drive from just outside the Saint Etienne penalty area to put the Reds back into the lead. Liverpool, however, needed to win by two clear goals to win the tie, as Saint Etienne's away goal would count double in the event of the aggregate scores remaining level at the end of the game.

Liverpool boss, Bob Paisley, sent on David Fairclough with fifteen minutes remaining as the Reds pressed forward for the decisive third goal. With just six minutes left, Fairclough latched on to a pass from Kennedy, sped past three defenders and shot past the Saint Etienne goalkeeper to score the greatest goal of his Liverpool career. Anfield went berserk as Liverpool held on to their two-goal cushion for a famous victory.

Emlyn Hughes described the victory against Saint Etienne as one of the finest of his Liverpool career.

Liverpool: Clemence, Neal, Jones, Smith, Kennedy, Hughes, Keegan, Case, Heighway, Toshack (Fairclough), Callaghan.
Saint Etienne: Curkovic, Janvion, Farison, Merchadier (H. Revelli), Lopez, Bathenay, Rocheteau, Larque, P.Revelli, Synaeghel, Santini.

Liverpool 0 West Ham United 0
Football League First Division, Anfield, 14 May 1977
Emlyn Hughes lifted his second Football League Championship as captain after this 0-0 draw with West Ham at Anfield in May 1977. Only a point was needed to make certain of the title and this they

duly achieved despite the occasional scare from Trevor Brooking and company.

Emlyn Hughes was Liverpool's top performer on the day. His unlimited supply of energy was never more evident than in this game when he covered every blade of grass at the back for the Reds to make certain that the West Ham attack did not spoil Liverpool's party.

The queues to get into Anfield started from daybreak and by kick-off the gates had been closed for several hours. Liverpool were going for the first leg of a treble of major trophies, the FA Cup final against Manchester United and European Cup final against Borussia Moenchengladbach still to come. Liverpool fans also came to witness the final Anfield performance of their hero Kevin Keegan who was expected to move abroad after the European Cup final.

As it turned out, Keegan and his team did not have one of their better days, but the 0-0 draw gave Liverpool the title and to the Anfield faithful that was all that mattered. West Ham had their chances to win the game through Robson and Taylor. Kevin Keegan also hit a post and West Ham goalkeeper, Mervyn Day made several fine saves. At the end both teams seemed happy with the draw. Liverpool had won the title by one point from Manchester City with Ipswich a further five points back in third.

As an ecstatic Emlyn Hughes paraded the gleaming trophy around Anfield he was hopeful that he would be required to carry out this task on another two occasions before the 1976/77 season came to a close.

Liverpool: Clemence, Neal, Jones, Smith, Kennedy, Hughes, Keegan, Case, Heighway, Johnson (Fairclough), McDermott.
West Ham United: Day, Bonds, Lampard, Pike, Taylor, McGiven, Jennings, Robson, Devonshire, Brooking, Taylor.

Liverpool 3 Borussia Monchenglabach 1
European Cup final, Rome, 25 May 1977
On a fabulous evening in Rome Liverpool at long last won the European Cup. Emlyn Hughes' greatest desire was not to let down the many thousands of Liverpool fans who had made the long trek to

Rome after witnessing their team's disappointing FA Cup final defeat at Wembley against Manchester United just a few days earlier.

The German Champions were an accomplished team and in Berti Vogts Borussia had one of the finest defenders in world football. Kevin Keegan was determined to put Vogts and his fellow Borussia defenders to the sword in his final game for the Reds before moving to Hamburg for the following season. Keegan was at his imperious best as he gave the Borussia defence the run around throughout the entire ninety minutes.

Terry McDermott put Liverpool into the lead after twenty-eight minutes when he scored from a defence-splitting pass from Steve Heighway. Borussia hit back early in the second half when Simonsen latched onto a poor back pass from Case and beat Clemence with a superb strike into the top corner of the net.

Tommy Smith then restored Liverpool's lead with a great headed goal from a Heighway corner. Ray Clemence then had to make some crucial saves before Liverpool made the score 3-1 with eight minutes left on the clock. Kevin Keegan, who had been giving Berti Vogts a dog's life all evening, forced the German defender into giving away a penalty when he burst into the box only to be upended by the hapless Borussia defender. Phil Neal made no mistake from the spot-kick and the greatest night in Liverpool's history was complete.

As Emlyn Hughes stepped up to collect the European Cup he knew that this was probably the pinnacle of his outstanding career at Anfield

Liverpool: Clemence, Neal, Jones, Smith, Kennedy, Hughes, Keegan, Case, Heighway, Callaghan, McDermott.
Borussia Moenchengladbach: Kneib, Vogts, Klinkhammer, Wittkamp, Bonhof, Wohlers (Hannes), Simonsen, Wimmer (Kulik), Stielike, Schaeffer, Heynckes.

England 0 Switzerland 0
Friendly, Wembley, 7 September 1977
Emlyn Hughes captained what was predominantly a Liverpool side against Switzerland in this 1977 friendly against Switzerland at Wembley.

Fresh from winning the European Cup, seven of the Liverpool team that appeared in the final in Rome were selected by new England manager Ron Greenwood to take on the Swiss.

Kevin Keegan was now plying his trade for German club Hamburg, but he must have felt like he was walking into the home dressing room at Anfield when he turned up for the game. Terry McDermott was making his international debut. The other Liverpool players in the team were Ray Clemence, Phil Neal, Emlyn Hughes, Ray Kennedy and Ian Callaghan. Callaghan was making his first England appearance for eleven years.

Liverpool were undoubtedly an outstanding club side, the best in Europe. the smart question was how would a team built around Bob Paisley's all-conquering side perform on the international stage? The answer, if this display against Switzerland was anything to go by, was not very encouraging. England had enough chances to have won the game, but their display in general lacked drive and spark. The best of the Liverpool contingent was Ian Callaghan, but his age meant that he was never really going to be in Ron Greenwood's long-term plans. Terry McDermott also had a sound game on his debut and he went on to win twenty-five caps for his country.

Emlyn Hughes was obviously proud to have captained a Liverpool/England side against another country, but the experiment never really came off. Perhaps if Tommy Smith, Jimmy Case, Joey Jones and Steve Heighway had been there the result might have been better!

England: Clemence, Neal, Cherry, McDermott, Watson, Hughes, Keegan, Channon (Hill), Francis, Kennedy, Callaghan (Wilkins).
Switzerland: Burgener, Trinchero, Fischbach, Bizzl, Chapulsat, Haslor (Brechbuhl), Barberis, Elsener (Reider), Kutel (Suiser), Demarmels (von Wartburg), Botteron.

England 2 Italy 0
World Cup qualifier, Wembley, 16 November 1977
Emlyn Hughes was winning his fiftieth international cap when he captained England to this fine 2-0 victory over Italy at Wembley in 1977. Ron Greenwood had taken over from Don Revie as England

manager. Although the Italians looked virtually certain to qualify for the 1978 World Cup finals at the expense of England, the home team produced one of their best displays for years.

England had been drawn in a qualifying group with Italy, Finland and Luxembourg. In a group in which goal difference was everything, only the group leader going through, England failed to match Italy's goal tally. After the Wembley fixture Italy needed only to beat Luxembourg to deprive Greenwood's team of a place at the 1978 World Cup finals, which they duly did. It was still however a proud day for Emlyn Hughes when he led his country out for his fiftieth cap.

A 92,000 crowd packed into Wembley to witness how Greenwood's team would do against one of world football's finest teams. The answer was an emphatic thumbs-up as England produced an outstanding display to send the Wembley crowd home happy. England won 2-0 with goals from Kevin Keegan and Trevor Brooking.

England fielded three players winning their first caps, Coppell, Latchford and Barnes. All performed well in a fine all-round team display. Keegan's opening goal came when he ran into the box to dispatch a Brooking centre past Zoff with a firm header. The second goal came nine minutes from time when Steve Coppell set up Keegan who centered into the goalmouth for Brooking to sidefoot past Zoff. Although England's World Cup dreams were practically at an end, the Wembley crowd cheered Emlyn Hughes and his team from the field at the final whistle. The Greenwood era in England's football history was beginning to look distinctly promising.

England: Clemence, Neal, Watson, Hughes, Cherry, Coppell, Wilkins, Brooking, Barnes, Keegan (Francis), Latchford (Pearson). **Italy**: Zoff, Tardelli, Mozzini, Facchetti (Cuccuredu), Benetti, Gentile, Zaccarelli, Antognoni, Causio, Graziani (Sala), Bettega.

Benfica 1 Liverpool 2
European Cup quarter-final first leg, Lisbon, 1 March 1978
Emlyn Hughes scored Liverpool's winner in a crucial 2-1 victory against the champions of Portugal, Benfica, in this 1978 European Cup quarter-final first-leg tie.

Benfica were on a 46-game unbeaten run and the home team showed their class to taken an early lead. Sheu hit a long ball that Nene latched onto before neatly slotting his shot past Ray Clemence in the Liverpool goal.

The game was played in torrential rain and the surface of the pitch was waterlogged in places. The strength of the Liverpool midfield then began to come to the fore and the Reds equalised after thirty-seven minutes through Jimmy Case. Case was always capable of coming up with crucial goals for Liverpool in European competition and he came to the Reds' rescue again when his free-kick slid under the Benfica goalkeeper Bento's body and into the net.

In the second half Liverpool adjusted much better to the worsening conditions as the rain continued to make the playing surface more and more treacherous as the minutes ticked by. Benfica's bright start was now a fading memory as Liverpool ploughed through the mud to set up a series of goalscoring chances.

Emlyn Hughes winner came in the seventy-second minute when McDermott passed to Neal on the wing. Neal found Case who slotted the ball to Dalglish. Dalglish spotted that Hughes had joined the attack near the edge of the penalty area. He fed the ball to the Liverpool captain, who scooped in a cross from the left that floated over the Benfica goalkeeper and under the crossbar for a Liverpool winner. Whether it was a cross or a shot, Emlyn Hughes claimed that the ball had gone exactly where he intended it to and few disagreed. Liverpool had achieved a famous victory on the road to retaining the European Cup.

Benfica: Bento, Lopez (Pereirenta), Humberto, Alberto, Eurico, Pietra, Nene, Toni, Celso, Sheu (Wilson), Cavungi.
Liverpool: Clemence, Neal, Smith, Thompson (Hansen), Kennedy, Hughes, Callaghan, Case, Heighway, McDermott, Dalglish.

Liverpool I Bruges 0

European Cup final, Wembley, 10 March 1978

Emlyn Hughes held the European Cup aloft for the second time in his career after the victory over Bruges in the 1978 final at Wembley.

The Belgian Champions had to take on Liverpool without their two main forwards, Courant and Lambert. With this in mind they decided to play a defensive game, hoping to catch Liverpool on the break. Liverpool, however, were by now experts at adapting their gameplan to suit the occasion and the style of play of the opposition.

The final was like a chess match with neither team wanting to make the first fatal mistake. Paisley's men were patient and the first half finished all square, the only Liverpool chance of note coming when Hansen headed over the bar.

The beginning of the second half followed a similar pattern; Liverpool patiently probing away at the Bruges defence, but without much penetration. Bob Paisley then decided to send on Steve Heighway for Jimmy Case and the momentum of Liverpool's play stepped up a gear. Within a minute of Heighway coming on the Eire international found Terry McDermott who hit the ball to Dalglish. Dalglish hit the ball back to Souness and then made space for himself with a run into the Bruges penalty area. Souness sent a perfectly weighted through ball back to Dalglish, who delicately chipped the oncoming Bruges goalkeeper to put the Reds into the lead.

It was a superb goal and despite some anxious moments near the end, Liverpool held on for a famous victory. In many ways it was a non-event of a final, mainly due to the negative tactics employed by the Belgians.

Unbelievably, Emlyn Hughes had captained Liverpool to a second consecutive European Cup, a feat never emulated by a British footballer before or since.

Liverpool: Clemence, Neal, Thompson, Hansen, Kennedy, Hughes, Dalglish, Case (Heighway), Fairclough, McDermott, Souness.
Bruges: Jensen, Bastijns, Krieger, Leekens, Maes (Volders), Cools, De Cubber, Van der Eycken, Ku (Sanders), Simeon, Soerensen.

Denmark 3 England 4

European Championship qualifier, Copenhagen, 20 September 1978

Emlyn Hughes captained England to this sensational 4-3 victory over Denmark in a qualifying game for the 1980 European Championship Finals. Denmark had the former European Footballer of the Year Alan Simonsen in their line-up and although England were expected to leave Copenhagen with a vital victory in the bag, they knew that Simonsen and company were capable of giving them plenty of problems.

In Kevin Keegan, however, England had their very own superstar of European football. Keegan came in for some harsh treatment by the Danish defenders right from the start, mainly from his man-marker Lund. Keegan made Lund and the rest of his Danish teammates pay for their brutal tackling by scoring two goals in the first twenty-two minutes. Both of Keegan's goals came from headers and he could have had a quick fire hat-trick when another of his goalbound efforts struck a post and bounced to safety.

Alan Simonsen then began to make an impact on the game and put his team back into contention with a calmly taken penalty kick. The Copenhagen crowd then went berserk when Arnesun put Denmark level with a sweetly struck shot past Clemence. England were rattled and an unlikely defeat was not out of the question.

Trevor Brooking then came to the rescue when he set up England's third goal. After winning a corner Brooking received the ball and sent in a low cross that Bob Latchford scrambled over the line. It had been a pulsating game and there was plenty of excitement still to come. England pushed forward for a fourth goal and were rewarded when Phil Neal struck a powerful shot past Jensen for what they thought was the clinching goal. The Danes, however, refused to lie down and Rontwed gave them renewed hope when he hit a piledriver past Clemence just a minute after Neal's goal.

England held on for a 4-3 victory in one of the most exciting games of Emlyn Hughes' England career.

Denmark: Jensen, F. Nielsen, Jensen, Rontved, Lerby, Arnesen, C. Nielsen, Lund (Fortuna), Simonsen, B. Neilsen (Hansen), Kristensen.

England: Clemence, Neal, Hughes, Watson, Mills, Wilkins, Keegan, Brooking, Coppell, Latchford, Barnes.

Liverpool 2 Ipswich Town 0
Football League First Division, Anfield, 24 March 1979

Emlyn Hughes' last League game for Liverpool was on 24 March 1979 against Ipswich Town. After 474 League appearances and 35 goals for the Reds, he bowed out in this 2-0 victory that kept Liverpool on course for yet another League title. Hughes did play for Liverpool again in the FA Cup defeat against Manchester United early in April at Goodison Park, but his departure to Wolves soon afterwards brought his Anfield career to a close.

Emlyn Hughes played at left-back for his final League game and gave a solid display against the talented Ipswich attack of Muhren, Mariner and Woods. Ipswich were one of the First Division's better sides throughout the 1970s and usually finished among the top four in the table.

Kenny Dalglish was Liverpool's star man on this particular March afternoon in 1979. It was Dalglish who opened the scoring for the Reds when Terry Butcher failed to cut out a McDermott cross. Dalglish kept his cool to place the ball calmly past Cooper for Liverpool's first goal.

Liverpool, despite never really getting into top gear, kept a firm grip on the game throughout. Mariner came close for Ipswich with a header that beat Ray Clemence in the Liverpool goal but sailed inches wide of the post.

Kenny Dalglish had given Terry Butcher and his fellow Ipswich defenders a torrid time all afternoon and it was no surprise when he set up David Johnson for the clinching goal with a low cross for the striker to score from close range.

As the 43,000 inside Anfield applauded their team off at the end, few people inside the ground realised that they had just witnessed the final appearance on home soil of Emlyn Hughes. Hughes had become almost part of the furniture at Anfield. It was obvious that his days in the red of Liverpool were numbered, but it still came as a shock when it finally dawned on the Anfield faithful that the days of witnessing 'Crazy Horse' giving his all for the team had gone forever.

Liverpool: Clemence, Neal, Hughes, Thompson, Kennedy, Hansen, Dalglish, Johnson, Case, McDermott, Souness.
Ipswich Town: Cooper, Burley, Tibbett (Brazil), Thijssen, Osman, Butcher, Wark, Muhren, Mariner, Mills, Woods.

Manchester United 1 Liverpool 0
FA Cup semi-final replay, Goodison Park, 4 April 1979

This was Emlyn Hughes' last game for his beloved Liverpool. Unfortunately it ended in defeat to Manchester United after the first game, played at Maine Road, had ended in a 2-2 draw.

The prize at stake was a place in the 1979 FA Cup final, a game that would have been a fitting climax to Emlyn Hughes' sensational career at Anfield. As it turned out, Hughes signed for Wolves soon after this FA Cup semi-final replay defeat and Reds fans, apart from his testimonial game, were never to witness Emlyn in the red of Liverpool again.

The only change that Bob Paisley made from the first game against United was to bring in Steve Heighway for Jimmy Case who started the game on the substitutes' bench.

Liverpool, as had been the case in the Maine Road game, began the match as firm favourites. They already looked certainties to collect yet another League title and were considered to be a far superior team to the Old Trafford outfit. The FA Cup, however, often sees the form book overturned and United had plenty of potential match-winners in their line-up. Ray Clemence had to be at his brilliant best to keep out Coppell, Macari and Jordan as United pressed for the first goal. Jordan also hit the Liverpool crossbar with a header. Ray Kennedy then hit the United woodwork with a rasping shot.

Liverpool's midfield then began to take control of the game in the second half with Graeme Souness dictating matters. It looked only a matter of time before Liverpool would take the lead, but it was to be United who would strike the first and only goal of the game. With just ten minutes left on the clock, Mickey Thomas crossed into the Liverpool penalty area where Jimmy Greenhoff had given Emlyn Hughes the slip. Greenhoff kept his cool and calmly headed past the advancing Clemence to give his team a famous victory.

After numerous victorious nights in the colours of Liverpool, Emlyn Hughes sadly left the pitch at Goodison Park on the losing side. It was a feeling that he had rarely experienced during Liverpool's triumphant trophy-winning decade of the 1970s.

Manchester United: Bailey, Nicholl, Albiston, McQueen, Buchan, McIlroy, Macari (Richie), Thomas, Coppell, Greenhoff, Jordan.
Liverpool: Clemence, Neal, Hughes, Thompson, Hansen, McDermott, Souness, Kennedy, Heighway, Dalglish, Johnson (Case).

Liverpool 3 Wolverhampton Wanderers 0
Football League First Division, Anfield, 3 November 1979

It seemed odd to see Emlyn Hughes run out at Anfield in the famous gold and black of Wolverhampton Wanderers on a cold November afternoon in November 1979. Hughes' great mentor, Bill Shankly, sat on the Wolves team coach as it drove to Anfield at the request of the former Liverpool captain on his return to his spiritual home. Liverpool were the reigning League Champions and even a player with the never-say-die spirit of Emlyn Hughes did not expect to take much from an encounter against Bob Paisley's outstanding team.

Hughes was given an emotional reception by the Anfield faithful when he took to the field. For the Liverpool team, however, there was no room for sentiment; it was business as usual as they took Wolves apart with a devastating second-half display of attacking football.

Kenny Dalglish put Liverpool in front as early as the third minute when Emlyn Hughes was unable to keep pace with Dalglish's devastating run into the box to slot the ball home. For the rest of the half, Hughes and his central defensive partner, George Berry, were made to look distinctly uneasy by Dalglish and David Johnson, as they probed for a second goal.

Early in the second half Dalglish struck again after superb build-up play by Neal, McDermott and Johnson. Dalglish latched on to Johnson's pass to stroke home Liverpool's second.

Andy Gray almost snatched one back for Wolves, only to see McDermott clear his goalbound effort off the line. In general, however,

Wolves were forced to mount a rearguard action to keep Liverpool from notching up double figures. Bradshaw in the Wolves goal had an outstanding, game pulling off a series of magnificent saves. Ray Kennedy wrapped up a comfortable victory for the Reds when he scored Liverpool's third near the end.

Emlyn Hughes had to endure an uncomfortable ninety minutes on his return to Anfield, but the warm reception that close on 50,000 packed into the ground gave him on his return to the scene of his past glories brought tears to his eyes.

Liverpool: Clemence, Neal, A. Kennedy, Thompson, R. Kennedy, Hansen, Dalglish, Case, Johnson, McDermott, Souness.
Wolverhampton Wanderers: Bradshaw, Palmer, Parkin, Patching, Hughes, Berry, Hibbitt, Carr, Gray, Richards, Thomas.

Wolverhampton Wanderers 1 Nottingham Forest 0
Football League Cup final, Wembley, 13 March 1980
In this match Emlyn Hughes achieved the only medal that was denied him during his glory days at Anfield.

Wolves' victory over Brian Clough's Nottingham Forest in March 1980 came after a hard-fought, energy-sapping match at Wembley. Forest were attempting to win the trophy for the third consecutive time.

Clough's team had been dealt a blow in the week leading up to the final when Emlyn Hughes' former Liverpool teammate Larry Lloyd was forced to sit out the game after receiving a one-match ban. Lloyd had pleaded his case with the FA, but his poor disciplinary record went against him and he missed the final.

Nottingham Forest were favourites to take the trophy, but Wolves fought like tigers to grind out a 1-0 victory. The winning goal came after sixty-seven minutes. Peter Shilton collided with David Needham in pursuit of a hopeful Wolves punt into the Forest penalty area. Andy Gray made the most of his good fortune and Shilton could only look on in horror as the Wolves striker tapped the ball into the unguarded net. Andy Gray and his strike partner John Richards had had precious few chances to test the Forest defence, but Wolves now found themselves with one hand on the trophy.

The remainder of the match saw Forest pounding away at Wolves in pursuit of an equaliser. Emlyn Hughes was superb, using his vast experience to marshal his defence against the oncoming red tide of Forest attacks. Wolves held out to win their second League Cup in six years.

Emlyn Hughes had finally won the one domestic medal that had eluded him throughout his Liverpool career. Andy Gray might have scored the winner, but Emlyn Hughes was the main catalyst of a rare trophy success for the Midlands club.

Wolverhampton Wanderers: Bradshaw, Palmer, Parkin, Daniel, Berry, Hughes, Carr, Hibbitt, Gray, Richards, Eves.
Nottingham Forest: Shilton, Anderson, Gray, McGovern, Needham, Burns, O'Neill, Bowyer, Birtles, Francis, Robertson.

Scotland 0 England 2

Home International Championship, Hampden Park, 24 May 1980
This was Emlyn Hughes last appearance for his country, Ron Greenwood bringing him on for his sixty-second cap in the second half.

Northern Ireland had actually won their first Home International Championship for the first time in sixty-six years, but Greenwood's team had their sights firmly set on a bigger prize. They were due to compete in the European Championship finals in Italy the following month, so the Home Internationals were regarded by Greenwood and the England team as no more than warm-up games for the main event. A game against Scotland at Hampden Park, however, is very rarely a friendly affair and both sides were determined not to finish bottom of the Home International table.

Emlyn Hughes knew that he had little chance of making Greenwood's squad for the Euro Championships, but he was still delighted to have gained another international cap in the twilight stage of his professional career. The selection of his former Anfield teammates Ray Clemence, Phil Thompson, David Johnson and Terry McDermott in the England team made Hughes feel at home for his final game for his country, with Thompson in fact captaining the side.

Scotland at the time were managed by Jock Stein and he sent his team out with the firm instructions that only a victory would be good enough. As expected, England ran out to face a hostile reception from the fanatical Scotland fans packed into Hampden Park. It was England, however, who seemed to be the more motivated team and they took an early lead through Brooking to silence the crowd. England pressed forward for more goals and only fine saves from Scotland goalkeeper Alan Rough kept the away team at bay.

In the second half England wrapped up the game when Steve Coppell beat Rough after good work by David Johnson and Trevor Brooking in the build-up. Emlyn Hughes was then brought on to replace Mariner for the remainder of the game. Hughes was under instructions to keep a firm grip on his former teammate Kenny Dalglish, a role that he accomplished with typical aplomb. Dalglish, the Scotland danger man, failed to get a kick for the rest of the game. Emlyn Hughes had carried out the task requested of him by Ron Greenwood to perfection.

Although he had failed to participate in the finals of a major international competition, Emlyn Hughes had been a magnificent servant to the national side. It was somehow fitting that his England career should end on a winning note.

Scotland: Rough, McCrain, Hegarty, Miller, Munro, Burley, Aitken, McLeish, Strachan, Dalglish, Jordan, Gemmill.
England: Clemence, Cherry, Thompson, Watson, Sansom, McDermott, Wilkins, Brooking, Coppell, Johnson, Mariner (Hughes).

Liverpool 1 Rotherham United 0
Football League (Milk) Cup, third round, Anfield,
11 November 1982
Another emotional return to Anfield for Emlyn Hughes, this time as player-manager of Rotherham United in an 1982 League Cup tie. Rotherham at the time were a Second Division side and Hughes had them well drilled in their pursuit of an unlikely cup upset at Anfield.

Rotherham were actually the better side for most of the game and were unlucky not to come away with at least a draw. Emlyn Hughes had a fine game for the Yorkshire team, marshalling his defence and keeping the Liverpool attack at bay with timely interceptions. Hughes said before the game that he had modelled his team's style of play on the Liverpool side of the 1970s. It was easy to see why they had challenged for promotion to the First Division in his first season in charge.

Both goalkeepers, Grobbelaar for Liverpool and Mountford for Rotherham, pulled off several fine saves in the first half. In the second period Grobbelaar was the busier of the two and kept the Reds in the game with fine saves from Seasman and McBride. Rotherham almost took the lead twelve minutes from time when Liverpool's defenders were relieved to see the ball hit the post before rebounding to safety after a goalmouth scramble.

Emlyn Hughes was confident that his team would hold out for at least a draw, but Liverpool's class came through in the end to spoil Rotherham's night. A defence-splitting pass from Graeme Souness found Craig Johnston, who ended Rotherham's dreams with the only goal of the game. Rotherham had put up a brave display, one that Emlyn Hughes could be proud of in his last competitive game at Anfield.

Liverpool: Grobbelaar, Neal, Kennedy, Thompson, Johnston, Hansen, Hodgson, Lee, Rush, Lawrenson, Souness.
Rotherham United: Mountford, Forrest, Breckin, Henson, Hughes, Green, Towner, Gooding, Moore, Seasman, McBride.

THE KEY MANAGERS

RON STUART

Kendal-born Ron Suart was the man who gave Emlyn Hughes his first-team chance at Blackpool. Born in 1920, Suart signed for Blackpool in 1939 from non-League Netherfield. He made his Blackpool debut in 1946 and played 104 times for the Lancashire club. His favoured position was centre half, but he was equally adept at full-back.

Suart left Blackpool in 1949 to sign for their Lancashire rivals, Blackburn Rovers. He made 176 appearances for Rovers between 1949 and 1954. The highlight of his Blackpool career was reaching Wembley in 1948. His team were beaten 4-2 by Manchester United in that year's FA Cup final. In 1947 Blackpool also challenged for the First Division title, finishing in fifth position, just seven points behind champions Liverpool.

Ron Suart's Blackburn career was confined to the Second Division and he ended his Football League playing days when he signed for non-League Wigan Athletic in 1955. Suart was Wigan's player-manager for the 1955/56 season before quitting the playing side of football to take over as manager of Scunthorpe United in 1956.

Suart achieved promotion with Scunthorpe in 1958, leading them into the Second Division as champions of the Third Division (North). It was the only silverware that Scunthorpe had ever won in their Football League history. Key to their success was the shrewd management of Ron Suart and the goalscoring exploits of their two strikers, Jack Haigh and Ron Waldock, throughout the 1957/58 campaign.

Ron Suart took over at Blackpool the following season and finished eighth in the First Division as well as reaching the quarter-finals of the FA Cup. Throughout the 1960s Blackpool never looked remotely like challenging for the game's major honours, but they always produced outstanding players. Gordon West, Jimmy Armfield, Alan Ball

and Emlyn Hughes are just some of the many talented players who
Suart managed during his Blackpool career. Alan Ball described Suart
as, 'A lovely man who encouraged me to enjoy my football and to
make things happen.' Emlyn Hughes described Suart as, 'A big, burly,
honest man that I would trust with my life.'

With Ball's departure to Everton in 1966 and Hughes to Liverpool
early in 1967, it was obvious that Blackpool were always going to be
a selling club and Ron Suart was never going to have the chance of
turning them into a leading side.

Suart was sacked by Blackpool in 1967 after the club were relegated
from the First Division. He then began a sixteen-year period in the
employment of Chelsea Football Club, first as assistant manager to Tommy
Docherty and then taking over from Dave Sexton as boss in 1974.

Suart's first season in charge saw Chelsea relegated to the Second
Division in 1975. Eddie McCreadie then became manager with Suart
becoming the general manager at Stamford Bridge. He remained as
general manager at Chelsea until 1978, when he was appointed chief
coach until 1983. In the early 1990s Ron Suart was still involved in
football as chief scout for Wimbledon.

BILL SHANKLY

Bill Shankly was the legendary Liverpool manager who saw Emlyn
Hughes make his debut for Blackpool against Blackburn Rovers in
May 1966 and tried to sign the teenager there and then.

Shankly was born in Glenbuck in 1913 and came from a family
of professional footballers. He signed professional forms for Carlisle
United in 1932 and after only 16 appearances moved to Second
Division Preston North End in 1933.

Bill Shankly was an all-action midfielder who never knew when
he was beaten. He was a key member of the Preston team that won
promotion to the First Division in 1934. Shankly was an FA Cup
winner at Preston in 1938 when his team beat Huddersfield Town
in the final. He also received a loser's medal in the 1937 final when
Sunderland beat Preston at Wembley.

His most successful season in the League was in 1938 when Preston finished third, two points behind Wolves and three behind Champions Arsenal. Bill Shankly was awarded five caps by Scotland and he made another seven appearances in wartime internationals. Shankly made 296 appearances for Preston, scoring 18 goals between 1933 and 1948.

When he retired as a player he accepted Carlisle United's offer to become their manager in 1949. Carlisle progressed under Shankly and finished third in the Third Division (North) in 1951.

Grimsby Town then offered Shankly the manager's job at Blundell Park at the start of the 1951/52 season. Grimsby were pipped for promotion to the Second Division by three points by champions Lincoln City. The following season Grimsby were in the frame for promotion again but fell away near the end of the campaign.

In January 1954, Bill Shankly took over at Third Division Workington Town, his main objective being to help them maintain their Football League status. The Shankly magic worked again as he moved them away from the foot of the table and into a more respectable League position.

Second Division Huddersfield Town approached Bill Shankly in 1955 to become assistant manager to Andy Beattie at Leeds Road. Shankly accepted and when Beattie was sacked a year later the Scot replaced him as manager. Bill Shankly remained at Huddersfield until 1959 and guided the development of future world-class stars Denis Law and Ray Wilson.

The finances were never really available at Huddersfield to achieve Shankly's aim of turning them into a top Second Division team capable of gaining promotion to the top flight. When Liverpool came calling in 1959, Bill Shankly knew it was an opportunity too good to refuse.

The signing of key players such as Ron Yeats, Gordon Milne and Ian St John turned Liverpool into a force to be reckoned with and they regained their First Division status in 1962. Within two seasons they were First Division Champions as the Shankly revolution at Anfield moved into top gear.

Further success followed as the FA Cup, two more League titles and the UEFA Cup found their way into the Anfield trophy cabinet. By the time Bill Shankly retired in 1974 he had developed an exciting new team at Liverpool, built around stars of the 1960s such as Tommy Smith and Ian Callaghan and outstanding new talent in the shape of Ray Clemence, Kevin Keegan and Emlyn Hughes.

It was Shankly's belief in Emlyn Hughes that got the raw teenager through a rocky initial period at the club and turned him into an international-class star. Emlyn Hughes, with his all-action style and never-say-die spirit was virtually Bill Shankly on the pitch. Emlyn Hughes kept up his strong friendship with Bill Shankly until the great man died in 1981.

SIR ALF RAMSEY

Dagenham-born Alf Ramsey was the greatest manager that the England international team have ever had.

Ramsey awarded Emlyn Hughes his first international cap against Holland in 1969. Although Hughes failed to play a single game in the 1970 World Cup finals in Mexico, Ramsey picked the Liverpool star on a regular basis until he lost the England manager's job in 1974.

Alf Ramsey's career in professional football began at Southampton in 1944. Prior to that he had played as an amateur for Portsmouth and his prowess at full-back had impressed the Saints when he played against them with an Army side in 1943. Ramsey was a classy defender who refused just to boot the ball clear, preferring to find a colleague with a precision pass instead. Ramsey played 90 times for Southampton, scoring 8 goals before signing for Tottenham Hotspur in 1949.

Alf Ramsey made his international debut for England in 1948, having an outstanding game in a 6-0 win against Switzerland at Highbury. He went on to win 32 caps, which was quite a large number considering he didn't win his first one until relatively late in his career.

The fee that Spurs paid for Ramsey, £21,000, was a British record at the time. Alf Ramsey was a key factor in Spurs' successful Second Division campaign in 1949/50 when they won the title. The following year saw the London club win the First Division Championship for the first time in their history, Spurs taking the title by four points from Manchester United. The following season saw Spurs once again fighting for the championship, finishing second, four points behind Matt Busby's side.

Alf Ramsey left Spurs in 1955 after 226 appearances for the club, scoring 24 goals, mostly from the penalty spot. He became manager at Ipswich Town in 1955 and against all the odds won the First Division Championship with them in 1962. Prior to that he had taken Ipswich to the Third Division (South) title in 1957 and the Second Division Championship in 1961. Ramsey was clearly an outstanding manager and after Ipswich's fantastic title-winning season of 1961/62 he was offered the England manager's job early in 1963. England's World Cup victory of 1966 was the pinnacle of Ramsey's career and he will forever be an immortal figure to England football fans. The secret of his success was his fine tactical brain and the close relationship he had with his players. He was loyal to them and in return they gave their all for the England boss.

Early in his England career Emlyn Hughes displeased Alf by staying out a little longer than the England boss had instructed. The following day Ramsey collared Hughes and told him, 'You'll do as I say or you'll be on the next plane home. Now piss off.' Emlyn never stayed out late again and for Ramsey the matter was closed.

Hughes was as shocked and angry as many of Ramsey's men were when the FA sacked him in 1974. England had failed to qualify for the 1974 World Cup finals and Ramsey took the blame. In 113 matches under Alf Ramsey England had suffered just 17 defeats.

In 1976, Ramsey, despite a more glamorous offer from Ajax, joined the board at Birmingham City. He became manager in 1977, but poor health caused him to retire from football after only six months in the job. Ill health continued to dog Ramsey and after suffering a stroke in 1998 he died in a nursing home the following year.

BOB PAISLEY

Bob Paisley was the manager who turned Liverpool's and Emlyn Hughes' European Cup dreams into a reality.

Paisley was born in Hetton-le-Hole in 1919. His playing career began with Bishop Auckland in 1938. In 1939 he won an FA Amateur

Cup winner's medal with Bishop Auckland before joining Liverpool just before the start of the war.

Paisley was a strong-running wing half who possessed the heart of a lion along with a stinging tackle. He won a League Championship medal in 1947 after Liverpool narrowly won the 1946/47 First Division title from Manchester United and Wolves, both just a single point behind them in second and third. After scoring the winning goal against Everton in the 1950 FA Cup semi-finals, Paisley found himself surplus to requirements when he was left out of the team for the FA Cup final against Arsenal. It was the most disappointing moment of Bob Paisley's playing career.

Bob Paisley retired from playing in 1953 after making 253 appearances for Liverpool, scoring 10 goals. Paisley then joined the coaching staff at Anfield and Bill Shankly made him his assistant when he joined the club in 1959. Paisley knew the game inside out and formed a formidable partnership with Shankly. They turned Liverpool into a major football force in the 1960s. When Bob Paisley was asked to succeed Shankly as Liverpool manager in 1974, he was at first slightly reluctant to take over the reins at Anfield. After taking a season to find his feet, there was then no stopping the Paisley trophy-winning machine as he won a sackful of major cups.

Emlyn Hughes had been appointed captain of Liverpool during Shankly's last season at the club and Bob Paisley was happy for that arrangement to continue. Emlyn Hughes might have shed tears when Bill Shankly handed in his notice, but like most of his teammates at Anfield he had a deep affection for Bob Paisley. When questioned after clinching the championship at Wolves in the final game of the 1975/76 season, Hughes told the press that he dedicated Liverpool's title win to his manager.

Even greater success was to follow under Paisley's management when he won three European Cups, two of them with Emlyn Hughes as skipper. Liverpool's defeat of Borussia Moenchengladbach in the 1977 European Cup final in Rome was probably Bob Paisley's greatest achievement as the Reds' manager.

The following year Liverpool retained the trophy at Wembley with a 1-0 victory over Bruges. By the time Paisley won his third European Cup in 1981 with a 1-0 defeat of Real Madrid, Emlyn Hughes was plying his trade for Wolves.

Bob Paisley decided to retire as Liverpool manager in 1983, but remained at Anfield to assist Joe Fagan and later Kenny Dalglish as an adviser. Paisley was also on the board at Liverpool until his retirement in 1992, when his health began to deteriorate. He had given the club forty-four years' service. Bob Paisley died after a long period of illness on St Valentine's Day 1996.

JOHN BARNWELL

John Barnwell gave Emlyn Hughes the opportunity to continue as a top-flight player when Liverpool decided that Hughes' best days were behind him in 1979.

Barnwell was born in Newcastle in 1938. Like Bob Paisley, Barnwell's career began at Bishop Auckland. He was snapped up by Arsenal in 1956. The midfield player won caps for the England Youth team while at Bishop Auckland and at Arsenal he was selected for the England Under-21 side. Barnwell played for Arsenal between 1956 and 1963, making 138 appearances and scoring 23 goals.

In 1963 he signed for Nottingham Forest and remained at the club until 1969. The highlight of Barnwell's Forest career came in 1967 when his team finished the 1966/67 campaign as runners-up to Manchester United in the First Division. Forest were four points behind Matt Busby's side, on the same number of points as third-placed Tottenham Hotspur. After 180 appearances and 22 goals for Nottingham Forest John Barnwell moved to Sheffield United in 1970, but played just 9 games for the club, scoring 2 goals.

Barnwell then took up coaching positions with Hereford United for three months, and then Peterborough United from 1972 until 1977. Peterborough then appointed John Barnwell as their manager in 1977. Peterborough failed, on goal average, to gain promotion to the Second Division in his first season in charge, but he was clearly a manager with potential.

After resigning from Peterborough in 1978, Barnwell applied for the vacant manager's post at Wolverhampton Wanderers. In November 1978 he moved in at Molineux and almost took the team to the FA

Cup final in his first season in charge. Arsenal knocked Wolves out of the competition at the semi-final stage.

Disaster then struck for the young up-and-coming manager when he sustained a fractured skull in a car accident. After recovering from his injuries, he returned to Molineux for the beginning of the 1979/80 season with the recently recruited Emlyn Hughes leading the side. John Barnwell had tremendous confidence in Hughes' ability to inspire the Wolves team and in Hughes' first season at the club they finished sixth in the League and won the Football League cup. Emlyn Hughes was enjoying an Indian summer at the tail end of his momentous career. John Barnwell remained at Wolves until 1982 when he refused an ultimatum from the chairman at Molineux to accept a set of new terms and conditions. Wolves were relegated and Barnwell was on the lookout for a new opportunity in football.

After spells abroad in Saudi Arabia, and also as manager of AEK Athens, Barnwell returned to English football in 1987. He became manager at Notts County but only lasted eighteen months at the club. Notts County reached the Third Division play-offs in Barnwell's first season at Meadow Lane, but millionaire chairman Derek Pavis was hungry for quick success and John Barnwell was replaced by Neil Warnock at the beginning of 1989.

John Barnwell then became the manager of Walsall early in 1989. At the time Walsall were deep in relegation trouble. Barnwell failed to halt Walsall's slide into the Third Division and when they were relegated the following year into the Fourth Division he found himself out of a job again.

SEASON-BY-SEASON SUMMARY FOR LIVERPOOL AND ENGLAND

1966/67

Emlyn Hughes was joining the reigning League Champions when he signed for Liverpool in February 1967. Some of Bill Shankly's team, however, had reached the peak of their football careers and Hughes was joining a side that would need re-building before too long.

Emlyn Hughes made his debut against Stoke City on 4 March and Liverpool won 2-1. Hughes was cup-tied for the FA Cup clash against Everton at Goodison Park seven days later and watched from the bench as his former Blackpool teammate, Alan Ball, scored the only goal of the game.

In Europe Liverpool's second tilt at the European Cup had ended well before Hughes joined the Reds. Inspired by the brilliant Johan Cruyff, Ajax dumped the Reds out of the competition before Christmas, 7-3 on aggregate.

With Liverpool trailing Manchester United in the race for the 1966/67 League title, Emlyn Hughes spent the remaining weeks of his initial period at Anfield trying to help his team close the gap on their Old Trafford rivals. Five defeats in their final eleven games, however, put paid to Liverpool's championship aspirations. Manchester United won the championship by four points from Nottingham Forest and Spurs, both tied on 56 points. Shankly's team finished a disappointing fifth in the table, nine points behind United. Emlyn Hughes had played in ten of the remaining matches. He had come to Anfield to win trophies, but he was destined to have a six-year wait before picking up his first medal with Liverpool.

Bill Shankly spent the summer months preparing for the coming season. Anfield favourite, Gordon Milne, was sold to Emlyn Hughes' old club Blackpool and Tony Hateley was purchased from Chelsea for a club record fee of £96,000. A more significant Shankly signing at the time, however, was the £18,000 paid to Scunthorpe for their young goalkeeper Ray Clemence.

Emlyn Hughes was delighted to have joined Liverpool, but for the time being he was not, as he had expected, now a member of the best team in the land. His joy at joining the Reds was also tempered by the fact that his old club Blackpool were relegated at the end of the 1966/67 season.

1967/68

Emlyn Hughes began the 1967/68 season with the no.6 shirt on his back. It became synonymous with Emlyn Hughes throughout his Liverpool career and it was only in his final games for the club in 1979 that he switched to no. 3. The previous owner of the no.6 jersey was Willie Stevenson and Willie played just four more games for the Reds before joining Stoke City in December 1968. Emlyn made the left-sided berth in the team his own during the new campaign and quickly became a crowd favourite.

The massive fee that Bill Shankly paid for Tony Hateley looked like it was money well spent as he cracked in a bagful of goals. Emlyn Hughes played in Europe for the first time in his career in the European Fairs Cup. After beating Munich 8-0 in an early round of the competition, Hughes must have wondered what all the fuss about European opposition was about. Shankly's side were brought back down to earth with a bump in the next round when Hungarian side Ferencvaros knocked the Reds out in two games played on snowy surfaces.

A good run in the FA Cup also came to an end when West Bromwich Albion put the Reds out of the competition after a second replay. The game, played at Manchester City's Maine Road, saw the Midlands team run out 2-1 winners.

It was in the race for the First Division Championship that Liverpool looked to have their greatest chance of success. After initially looking a world beater, Tony Hateley struggled to keep up his goalscoring ratio in League matches. In the FA Cup he had knocked in 8 goals in 7 matches; in the League it was a tally of 16 in 38 games.

Initially it looked like Manchester United would retain their crown, but Liverpool, Leeds and Manchester City were all in with a chance in the final weeks of the season.

Sloppy defeats against Sheffield United at home and West Ham and Stoke away put paid to Liverpool's title ambitions. The Joe Mercer and Malcolm Allison managerial double act at Manchester City ended up bringing the League title to Maine Road for only the second time in City's history. Manchester United finished second, two points behind City and Liverpool were a point behind United in third place. Shankly's team had come close, but the Hateley-Hunt pairing up front for the Reds was not deemed by Shankly to have been an unqualified success and he sold Hateley to Coventry City for £80,000 early in the following season.

For Emlyn Hughes the 1967/68 season had been one in which he firmly established himself as one of the key players that Bill Shankly would construct his next great team around.

Although Bill Shankly was delighted to see his great friend Matt Busby win the European Cup at Old Trafford, it further intensified the Liverpool manager's great desire to see his own team beating the best in Europe on a regular basis.

1968/69

Wolverhampton Wanderers striker Alun Evans was purchased by Bill Shankly at the beginning of the 1968/69 season for £100,000. It was a record fee for a teenager. Evans looked the business, scoring on his home debut against Leicester City in September after missing the early weeks of the new season through injury. When Evans scored a further two goals in a 6-0 thrashing of Wolves at Molineux a week later, it looked like a new Anfield star was born. Alun Evans' goalscoring form was short lived, however, and he only netted 7 goals in 33 League appearances during the 1968/69 season.

In Europe, Emlyn Hughes netted his first goal against European opposition when he scored Liverpool's second in a 2-1 victory against

Athletic Bilbao at Anfield. With the scores level at 2-2 on aggregate, Liverpool went out of the competition on the toss of a coin.

In the FA Cup, Leicester City drew with Liverpool at Filbert Street 0-0 and then came to Anfield and unexpectedly won the replay 1-0. That old Leicester FA Cup hoodoo had struck again.

In the League Liverpool once again mounted a strong challenge. Don Revie's Leeds United were now at their brilliant best and were aiming to win the title for the first time in their history. They lost only two League games all season and it was no surprise to see them win the championship by six points from Liverpool. Everton were four points behind the Reds in third spot.

Shankly's team had finished trophyless again and veterans of Liverpool's two title-winning sides of 1964 and 1966 such as St John and Hunt were nearing the end of theor Anfield careers. Gerry Byrne had had to retire from the game altogether through injury.

In any other season, Shankly's team would have probably won the League title with their 61-point total. Leeds United, however, were a formidable outfit and it would have needed something quite spectacular from Liverpool to have denied the Yorkshire side their first League Championship.

One record that Liverpool did create in the 1968/69 season was their defensive performance of conceding just 24 goals. Tommy Lawrence, Chris Lawler, Tommy Smith, Gerry Byrne and Ron Yeats were the most impressive defensive unit in the League at the time. Emlyn Hughes switched between defence and attack with consummate ease and it was around this time that England boss Alf Ramsey began to see a role for the young Liverpool player in the England set-up.

Bill Shankly prepared for the coming season by snapping up centre half Larry Lloyd from Bristol Rovers for a £50,000 fee. He also brought in Alec Lindsay from Bury for £67,000. Both were destined to become outstanding performers for the Reds in the years to come.

1969/70

This was the season when Emlyn Hughes achieved his boyhood ambition of playing for the England side. Alf Ramsey selected him for the 5 November 1969 game against Holland in Amsterdam. A goal from Colin Bell gave England a 1-0 victory. Everton, with their outstanding midfield trio of Ball, Harvey and Kendall, looked like they would be Leeds United's main challengers for their championship crown. Emlyn Hughes was in fine goalscoring form for Liverpool from his midfield berth this season, scoring 7 times in 41 League appearances.

In Europe, Shankly's side once again competed in the European Fairs Cup and an opening-round victory over Dundalk by a 14-0 aggregate margin gave them hopes of a successful campaign. The Reds came unstuck in the next round however when Portugal's Vitoria Setubal knocked them out on the away goals rule after the match finished up with a 3-3 aggregate scoreline from the two legs.

In the FA Cup a 1-0 defeat at Watford was the catalyst for Bill Shankly to admit that his great 1960s team had finally had their day. Callaghan, Smith and Lawler would be the only remnants of the 1960s side when Liverpool won their next League title in 1973.

Emlyn Hughes picked up further England caps against Portugal, Belgium, Wales, Northern Ireland and Scotland. He looked a cert to be in Alf Ramsey's squad for the 1970 World Cup finals, to be held in Mexico. His appearance against Northern Ireland was something special, it being Bobby Charlton's 100th England appearance.

In the race for the League Championship, Liverpool failed to mount a challenge, finishing a massive 15 points behind title winners Everton. Even second-placed Leeds could only manage to cut Everton's lead to nine points. Bill Shankly had some massive rebuilding to do if Liverpool were to usurp Everton's crown as Kings of Merseyside.

A lot of the players that would be introduced into the Liverpool first team in the coming season were already at Anfield, learning the Liverpool way in the reserve team. Ray Clemence, Brian Hall, Larry Lloyd, Alec Lindsay, John McLaughlin and newcomers Steve Heighway and John Toshack would all become first-team regulars in the new season.

At the 1970 World Cup finals, Emlyn Hughes returned home from Mexico without making an appearance for the reigning World Cup holders. After wins against Romania and Czechoslovakia and a defeat against eventual winners Brazil, England reached the quarter-finals. Emlyn Hughes could only sit on the England bench and watch as Ramsey's team threw away a two-goal lead against West Germany and ended up losing 3-2.

After that game Sir Alf Ramsey rarely left Hughes out of the England team.

1970/71

Bill Shankly's rebuilding of the team was beginning to take shape. The average age of the new Liverpool line-up was just twenty-two. When Shankly spent £110,000 on bringing in Cardiff striker John Toshack early in November 1970, the twenty-one-year-old joined a whole host of talented young players who would emerge as Shankly's next great team.

Tommy Smith was now the Liverpool skipper and other local lads Ian Callaghan and Chris Lawler were still at the top of their form. Great Liverpool servants of the 1960s such as St John, Yeats and Lawrence had come to the end of their Anfield careers. Alun Evans had not been a great success at Anfield, though he did score a fabulous hat-trick against Bayern Munich in Liverpool's encounter against the Germans early in 1971.

Liverpool came up against Leeds in the semi-final of the Fairs Cup and Revie's team proved to be too good for the Reds. Billy Bremner scored the only goal of the game in the first leg at Anfield. In the return leg, Leeds held on for a 0-0 draw to put Liverpool out. Bill Shankly's barren spell in Europe continued.

Emlyn Hughes picked up more international caps against East Germany, Malta, Greece and Wales during the 1970/71 season. For Liverpool he had his best chance yet of winning a trophy as the Reds fought their way through to the 1971 FA Cup final. Liverpool knocked out some tough opposition on their way to Wembley, most notably

League Champions Everton and a rejuvenated Spurs side. Liverpool's FA Cup semi-final 2-1 defeat of Everton came courtesy of goals from Brian Hall and Alun Evans.

Emlyn Hughes' first Wembley final was to end in disappointment with a Charlie George goal giving Arsenal the League and Cup double. Liverpool's new wing sensation, Steve Heighway, scored the first goal of the final, but Eddie Kelly equalised for Arsenal. The game went into extra time and Charlie George scored the most famous goal of his Highbury career to give his side a 2-1 victory. Bill Shankly was building a fine young side, but their League form still left a lot to be desired. Arsenal won the First Division title by a single point from Leeds, Liverpool trailing 14 points behind in fifth place.

Liverpool still needed a player to galvanise the team as an attacking force. Prior to the FA Cup final Bill Shankly signed the man who would do just that – his name was Kevin Keegan. Keegan was signed for a £35,000 fee from Scunthorpe United. It was an outstanding piece of transfer business by the canny Scot.

1971/72

The 1971/72 season was the campaign in which Liverpool went incredibly close to winning the League Championship for the first time since 1966. Kevin Keegan immediately fitted into the side and formed an outstanding attacking partnership with John Toshack. Ray Clemence and Alec Lindsay were also beginning to look like certain England internationals of the future. In the cup competitions, Liverpool's interest ended early, with Leeds knocking the Reds out of the FA Cup and Bayern Munich ending Shankly's European Cup-Winners' Cup hopes.

It was in the First Division that Liverpool emerged again as a potent force. Kevin Keegan looked sensational and Alf Ramsey had him playing for the England Under-23 side within months of his Liverpool debut. The race for the title was the most thrilling in years. Derby, Liverpool, Leeds and Manchester City were all still in with a chance in the final weeks of the season.

Liverpool had a fantastic run of fourteen victories from the end of January 1971 through to their 2-0 win over Ipswich at the end of April. The only hiccup was the point that they dropped away to Chelsea early in March. Their end-of-season form was sensational, then, right at the death, they dropped 3 points in their last 2 games. The crucial defeat was against eventual champions Derby County in the penultimate game of the season.

Liverpool could still have ended up as champions by winning at Highbury in their final game of the season, but Arsenal held them to a 0-0 draw. Leeds could also have taken the title by drawing at Wolves, but the Wolves goalkeeper Phil Parkes played the game of his life to keep Leeds out. Leeds lost 2-1 at Molineux.

Emlyn Hughes could have won Liverpool's encounter with Arsenal inside the first twenty minutes when he hit a superb thirty-yard volley that smashed against the crossbar. Hughes had still not won any silverware at Anfield, but all of that was about to change the following season.

Apart from his adventures with Liverpool as they challenged for the 1971/72 League title, Emlyn Hughes picked up further England caps with appearances against Switzerland, Greece, West Germany, Wales, Northern Ireland and Scotland during the season. Hughes, in fact, scored the only goal of his England career in the 3-0 victory over Wales in May. Colin Bell and Rodney Marsh scored the other two.

Bill Shankly prepared for the coming season by signing Peter Cormack for £110,000 from Nottingham Forest. Another key figure in the trophy-winning seasons that were soon to follow had been introduced into the Liverpool team. Phil Thompson had made 10 League appearances during the 1971/72 season, but would not become a permanent fixture in the Liverpool line-up until Shankly's final season at the club in the 1973/74 campaign.

1972/73

The 1972/73 season was the one in which Emlyn Hughes finally won his first medals as a Liverpool player.

Liverpool finished the campaign as League Champions and also won the UEFA Cup. In the First Division, Liverpool fought a three-horse race with Leeds and Arsenal. Football pundits had taken note of the outstanding young side that Bill Shankly had been building at Anfield during the previous few seasons and were not surprised to seem them now looking likely winners of the League Championship. Don Revie's Leeds United were still an outstanding team, but were now showing signs of being past their best.

The crunch game came on 23 April 1973. The Easter Monday encounter at Anfield between Liverpool and Leeds was virtually a championship shootout. Goals from Cormack and Keegan won the day for Liverpool. Emlyn Hughes had enjoyed another outstanding season playing in midfield for Liverpool, although England manager Alf Ramsey still selected him at left-back when it came to internationals. Kevin Keegan and Ray Clemence were also now England internationals.

Liverpool made sure of the First Division title with a 0-0 draw against Leicester City in their final game of the season. Tommy Smith had taken the Reds to his first League Championship as skipper of the side.

In Europe Liverpool had to get past Eintracht Frankfurt, AEK Athens, Dynamo Berlin, Dynamo Dresden, Tottenham Hotspur and finally Borussia Moenchengladbach to take the UEFA Cup. It was Bill Shankly's first and only European trophy as manager of Liverpool.

On the international scene, Emlyn Hughes secured further international appearances against Wales, Scotland, Poland, Russia and Italy. England's 5-0 victory over Scotland in Glasgow in February 1973 equalled England's highest ever score in an away game against the Scots.

1973/74

This was Bill Shankly's last season at Anfield and victory over Newcastle United in the 1974 FA Cup final saw him leave the club on a high note.

Emlyn Hughes' international appearances saw the team hit the highs and the lows in Sir Alf Ramsey's final months as England manager. A fine 7-0 victory over Austria at Wembley in September 1973 was followed by a disappointing 1-1 draw against Poland. The Poland game was the one that mattered, and failure to win meant that England lost virtually all hope of qualifying for the 1974 World Cup finals. Emlyn Hughes was destined to end his career without ever playing in the international game's major tournament.

Hughes won further caps during the 1973/74 season against Italy, Wales, Scotland, Argentina, East Germany, Bulgaria and Yugoslavia. Emlyn Hughes captained England for the first time in the 11 May Home International Championship game against Wales at Ninian Park. Goals from Bowles and Keegan gave England a 2-0 victory.

Liverpool's defence of their League Championship crown was put under the strongest test by Leeds United. Leeds would never have a team as good as the 1973/74 outfit ever again. Shankly's team was outstanding, but not even they could match Leeds when it came to the championship. Leeds won the League by five points from Liverpool, with Derby County nine points behind in third spot.

In Europe, Liverpool were outplayed by Red Star Belgrade. The Yugoslavians won both games 2-1 to take the tie 4-2 on aggregate. In the FA Cup Liverpool reigned supreme with victories over Doncaster, Carlisle, Ipswich, Bristol City and Leicester setting up an FA Cup final against Newcastle. The north-easterners were expected to provide stiff opposition, as their team was packed with talent. Bill Shankly's side however put on their finest display of the season to win the game 3-0. Kevin Keegan with two and Steve Heighway scored the goals, while Emlyn Hughes and Phil Thompson put on a defensive display at the heart of the Liverpool defence that gave a glimpse of what would help to conquer Europe in the years to come. An injury to Larry Lloyd earlier in the season had led Bill Shankly to pair Hughes and Thompson together at the heart of the Liverpool defence. Though neither were massive centre-backs in the Ronnie Yeats or Larry Lloyd mould, their elegant brand of defensive play became a benchmark for Liverpool's central defensive pairings in the years that followed.

Emlyn Hughes' first season as club captain had ended with him collecting the much coveted FA Cup at Wembley.

1974/75

Bob Paisley's first season in charge of Liverpool ended up trophyless. Bill Shankly had signed Ray Kennedy from Arsenal before his departure for a £200,000 fee. Bob Paisley himself brought in Phil Neal from Northampton Town for £66,000.

Liverpool's European ambitions ended early when, after an outstanding 11-0 victory over Norwegians Stromsgodset, Hungarians Ferencvaros put them out of the European Cup-Winners' Cup. Liverpool drew 1-1 at Anfield and then 0-0 in Hungary, but the away goals rule put Ferencvaros through. Ipswich put the Reds out of the FA Cup and Middlesbrough the League Cup. The latter, however, was a tournament that Liverpool were yet to show any real interest in.

Emlyn Hughes added to his England international cap collection with appearances against Czechoslovakia, Portugal, Cyprus and Northern Ireland. After the Ireland game, new England boss Don Revie decided to dispense with Emlyn Hughes for the next eighteen months.

In the First Division title race, half a dozen teams were still in contention as the season entered its climax. Some surprising names were still in with a shout such as Sheffield United, Stoke City and Middlesbrough. Eventual winners Derby County did not go top of the First Division until early in April. Liverpool blew their chance with defeats against Stoke and Middlesbrough in their final five games.

In the final week of the season, when Ipswich failed to take the points at Manchester City, Derby took the title with a game still to play. It was their second title win in four years. Liverpool finished in second place, just two points behind Derby.

When Liverpool had won the FA Cup against Newcastle the previous season, they looked like a side that would rule English football for years to come. Their failure to land a single trophy in Bob Paisley's first stint as manager led to some football commentators suggesting that perhaps he wasn't the right man to take over from Shankly. New signings Terry McDermott and Ray Kennedy were still taking a little time to settle into the Liverpool set-up. By the following season, however, Paisley's men were firing on all cylinders.

1975/76

This was a great season for Emlyn Hughes and his Liverpool team-mates, with two major trophies brought back to the Anfield trophy cabinet. Liverpool started the season badly in the League with a 2-0 defeat away to Queens Park Rangers. Liverpool then suffered only four more League defeats in the rest of the campaign.

Joey Jones, signed from Wrexham for £110,000, Jimmy Case and David Fairclough were all introduced into the Liverpool side in the 1975/76 season, but were not yet first-team regulars. David Fairclough produced some incredible match-winning performances for the Reds after coming on as a substitute, but he never really established himself as a regular choice in the team.

Queens Park Rangers, attempting to win the First Division title for the first time in their history, were Liverpool's main challengers for the championship. Manchester United and Derby also stayed near the top of the League throughout the season. Liverpool clinched the title with a 3-1 win at Wolves in the final game of the campaign. QPR were only a single point behind the Reds in second spot with Manchester United third.

Derby County knocked Liverpool out of the FA Cup in the fourth round and the Reds' League Cup aspirations (which were slim) ended early on in the competition when they lost to Burnley.

In the UEFA Cup victories over Hibernian, Real Sociedad, Slask Wroclaw, Dynamo Dresden and Barcelona put Liverpool into the two-legged final. Their opponents were Bruges. Liverpool beat Bruges 3-2 at Anfield and held the Belgians to a 1-1 draw in the second leg to take the UEFA Cup. It was Emlyn Hughes' first European trophy as captain of Liverpool. It was the second time that Liverpool had won the League and UEFA Cup double in three years. The modest Bob Paisley remarked, 'Bill Shankly set such a high standard. Liverpool have been geared up for this sort of thing for fifteen years. All I have done is help things along their way.'

Paisley prepared for an assault on the 1977 European Cup by signing striker David Johnson from Ipswich Town for a £200,000 fee.

1976/77

If the previous season had been outstanding, the 1976/77 campaign was quite spectacular for Bob Paisley's boys. The European Cup came to Anfield for the first time and the Reds also retained their League Championship crown. Liverpool almost completed an unprecedented treble of trophies, but lost to Manchester United in the FA Cup final.

Emlyn Hughes was also recalled to the England squad by Don Revie during the 1976/77 campaign. Another cause for personal celebration for the Liverpool skipper was being named Footballer of the Year.

Liverpool's title triumph made them the first club since Wolverhampton Wanderers in 1959 to retain the First Division Championship. Liverpool tasted defeat in just 2 of their opening 16 games, both by the odd goal to Birmingham and Newcastle. In the new year they went on a run of just 3 defeats in 20 games. Liverpool's closest challengers for the League title were Manchester City, Ipswich and Aston Villa. City lost out to Liverpool by just one point.

In the FA Cup, wins against Crystal Palace, Carlisle, Oldham, Middlesbrough and Everton took the Reds to Wembley for a showdown with Tommy Docherty's Manchester United. Liverpool had already beaten United in the League three weeks before the FA Cup final and were favourites to take the trophy. Goals from Stuart Pearson and Jimmy Greenhoff spoilt Liverpool's attempt to win the treble and they set off for the European Cup final in Rome a few days later determined to win the big prize.

Emlyn Hughes became the first Liverpool captain to lift the European Cup when goals from McDermott, Smith and Neal gave the Reds a 3-1 victory over Borussia Moenchengladbach in the 1977 final.

Most commentators regarded Liverpool's German opponents as top quality opposition. Bill Shankly begged to differ. The former Liverpool boss admitted that he was envious of Bob Paisley becoming the first Liverpool boss to bring Europe's major trophy back to Anfield. When it came to Borussia Moenchengladbach, Shankly claimed that most First Division teams would have given the Reds a tougher match. Shankly said, 'Winning the European Cup is supposed to be better than winning a domestic title, but most English clubs would have given Liverpool a better game than Borussia did tonight.'

The 1977 European Cup final was Kevin Keegan's last game for Liverpool and Bob Paisley went out and replaced him with a player who Emlyn Hughes regarded as even better, Kenny Dalglish. Paisley paid Celtic £440,000 for the Scottish international.

Emlyn Hughes increased his England international appearances tally during the 1976/77 season with caps against Italy, Luxembourg, Wales, Scotland, Brazil, Argentina and Uruguay.

1977/78

Liverpool began the 1977/78 season determined to become the first British club to win the European Cup in consecutive seasons. The way that Kenny Dalglish slotted into Kevin Keegan's place in the side, the omens were promising that Paisley's team would achieve their objective.

Emlyn Hughes had two defensive partners during the season. New signing Alan Hansen stood in for Phil Thompson for periods throughout the 1977/78 campaign when Thompson was injured. Hansen was signed by Bob Paisley for a £100,000 fee from Partick Thistle. The normally injury-free Hughes actually missed three League matches himself during the season, a rare occurrence for the Liverpool skipper. The first signs of his dodgy knee were beginning to show.

Nottingham Forest beat Liverpool to the League Championship by a seven-point margin, the Reds only really getting into their stride with an unbeaten 12-match run at the end of the season in the race for the title.

In the FA Cup, Chelsea knocked the Reds out in the third round, a 4-2 victory at Stamford Bridge. Liverpool, for the first time in their history, reached the final of the Football League Cup, a competition that they generally showed scant interest in. Once again it was Brian Clough's Nottingham Forest who denied the Reds some domestic silverware when they beat Liverpool 1-0 at Old Trafford, after the first game at Wembley had ended up 0-0.

Liverpool's defence of the European Cup was a much happier affair, with victories over Dynamo Dresden, Benfica and Borussia Moenchengladbach taking them to a Wembley final against Belgian Champions Bruges. Emlyn Hughes scored one of Liverpool's goals in the 2-1 victory away to Benfica in the Stadium of Light.

The final against Bruges was a tedious encounter, brought to life only by Kenny Dalglish's brilliant goal that gave the Reds a 1-0 victory. Bruges produced probably the most negative display of football ever witnessed in a European Cup final and this made Liverpool's victory all the more sweet. Emlyn Hughes lifted the European Cup for the second year in succession – it is doubtful that a Liverpool captain will ever again achieve this accolade.

Emlyn Hughes also achieved a personal milestone in international appearances during the 1977/78 campaign. After representing his country against Luxembourg in October 1977, the following month Hughes was in the England side that defeated Italy 2-0 at Wembley. It was his fiftieth appearance for his country. Emlyn Hughes won further caps against West Germany, Northern Ireland, Scotland and Hungary during the 1977/78 season.

1978/79

Emlyn Hughes' last season at Anfield was blighted by injuries. Alan Hansen and Phil Thompson were now Bob Paisley's preferred partnership at the heart of the Liverpool defence and when Hughes was in the side it was generally at full-back. The days of 'Crazy Horse' marauding from defence to attack were now a fading memory. When it came to playing at full-back, however, Emlyn Hughes was still a quality performer. Further international appearances proved testimony to Hughes' ability still to be a formidable performer in a defensive role. Emlyn Hughes made just 16 League appearances during the 1978/79 season, but it was still enough to qualify for his fourth First Division Championship medal.

Liverpool won the title by eight points from 1977/78 champions Nottingham Forest. West Bromwich Albion, unexpectedly, were just a point behind Forest in third spot. It was Bob Paisley's fortieth year at Anfield and his third League Championship as manager was fitting reward for decades of great service to Liverpool Football Club.

In the cup competitions Nottingham Forest continued to be Liverpool's bogey team when they knocked the Reds out of the European Cup in the first round of the competition. Emlyn Hughes played in both legs of the Forest tie, his last games for Liverpool in Europe. Liverpool also went out of the Football League Cup early on in the competition, to Sheffield United.

After wins against Southend, Blackburn, Burnley and Ipswich, Liverpool faced Manchester United in the FA Cup semi-final. The first game at Maine Road resulted in a 2-2 draw. In the replay at Goodison Park, Liverpool went out of the competition when a Jimmy Greenhoff goal won the game 1-0 for United. It was Emlyn Hughes' last appearance for Liverpool. New signing Alan Kennedy, a £300,000 recruit from Newcastle United, was not selected for the cup games against Manchester United, but Bob Paisley now knew that the left-back spot in the side was the property of the north-easterner for the foreseeable future. Emlyn Hughes was sold to Wolves at the end of the 1978/79 season.

Emlyn Hughes won further international caps against Denmark, Eire, Northern Ireland and Wales during his last season at Anfield.

APPENDICES

EMLYN HUGHES' LIVERPOOL RECORD

FOOTBALL LEAGUE 1966/67

March	4	(h)	Stoke City	W	2-1	Lawler 14, Hunt 62
	18	(a)	Burnley	L	0-1	
	25	(h)	Manchester United	D	0-0	
	28	(a)	Arsenal	D	1-1	Arrowsmith 68
April	7	(h)	Newcastle United	W	3-1	Hunt 48, 80, Callaghan 84
	22	(h)	West Bromwich Albion	L	0-1	
	28	(a)	Sheffield United	W	1-0	Hunt 82
May	3	(a)	Leeds United	L	1-2	Stevenson (pen) 23
	6	(h)	Tottenham Hotspur	D	0-0	
	13	(h)	Blackpool	L	1-3	Thompson 21

1967/68

August	18	(a)	Manchester City	D	0-0	
	22	(h)	Arsenal	W	2-0	Hunt 23, 75
	26	(h)	Newcastle United	W	6-0	Hateley 8, 47, 75, Hughes 30, Hunt 41, 87
	28	(a)	Arsenal	L	0-2	
September	2	(a)	West Bromwich Albion	W	2-0	Hateley 6, Hunt 58
	5	(a)	Nottingham Forest	W	1-0	Hughes 51
	9	(h)	Chelsea	W	3-1	Smith (pen) 37, Hateley 46, 47
	16	(a)	Southampton	L	0-1	
	23	(h)	Everton	W	1-0	Hunt 78
	30	(h)	Stoke City	W	2-1	Thompson 38, Smith 55
October	7	(a)	Leicester City	L	1-2	St John 27
	14	(h)	West Ham United	W	3-1	St John 15, 38, Smith 68
	24	(a)	Burnley	D	1-1	Lawler 82
	28	(h)	Sheffield Wednesday	W	1-0	Lawler 10
November	4	(a)	Tottenham Hotspur	D	1-1	Hunt 72
	11	(h)	Manchester United	L	1-2	Hunt 8
	18	(a)	Sunderland	D	1-1	Irwin (og) 26
	25	(h)	Wolves	W	2-1	Hateley 1, Stevenson (pen) 83
December	2	(a)	Fulham	D	1-1	Hateley 80
	9	(h)	Leeds United	W	2-0	Hunt 18, Sprake (og) 44

	16	(h)	Manchester City	D	1-1	Hunt 50
	23	(a)	Newcastle United	D	1-1	St John 43
	26	(a)	Coventry City	D	1-1	Hunt 13
	30	(h)	Coventry City	W	1-0	Callaghan 17
January	6	(h)	West Bromwich Albion	W	4-1	Strong 3,
						Hunt 57, 67, 79
	20	(h)	Southampton	W	2-0	Strong 55, Yeats 85
February	3	(a)	Everton	L	0-1	
	12	(a)	Chelsea	L	1-3	Thompson 80
	24	(h)	Leicester City	W	3-1	Callaghan 51,
						Strong 59, Hateley 78
March	2	(a)	Wolves	D	1-1	Hunt 79
	16	(h)	Burnley	W	3-2	Hateley 31, 73,
						Strong 61
	23	(a)	Sheffield Wednesday	W	2-1	Hunt 27, Arrowsmith 88
April	6	(a)	Manchester United	W	2-1	Yeats 9, Hunt 17
	12	(h)	Sheffield United	L	1-2	Hunt 32
	13	(h)	Sunderland	W	2-1	Hunt 18, 71
	15	(a)	Sheffield United	D	1-1	Strong (pen) 34
	20	(a)	West Ham United	L	0-1	
	27	(h)	Fulham	W	4-1	Callaghan 29,
						Hunt 40, 49, Hateley 56
	29	(h)	Tottenham Hotspur	D	1-1	Hateley 38

1968/69

August	10	(h)	Manchester City	W	2-1	Graham 24, Thompson 73
	14	(a)	Southampton	L	0-2	
	17	(a)	Arsenal	D	1-1	Hunt 50
	20	(h)	Stoke City	W	2-1	Callaghan 63, Allen (og) 75
	24	(h)	Sunderland	W	4-1	Smith 1, Lawler 16,
						Callaghan 44, Hateley 66
	27	(a)	Everton	D	0-0	
	31	(a)	Leeds United	L	0-1	
September	7	(h)	Queens Park Rangers	W	2-0	Yeats 43, Graham 55
	14	(a)	Ipswich Town	W	2-0	Graham 48, St John 89
	21	(h)	Leicester City	W	4-0	Yeats 2, Smith (pen) 4,
						Evans 10, Callaghan 12
	28	(a)	Wolves	W	6-0	Hunt 15, 74, Thompson 25,
						80, Evans 30, 63
October	5	(a)	Burnley	W	4-0	Hunt 20, 35,
						Thompson 62, Strong 87
	8	(h)	Everton	D	1-1	Smith 75
	12	(h)	Manchester United	W	2-0	St John 14, Evans 82
	19	(a)	Tottenham Hotspur	L	1-2	Hunt 37
	26	(h)	Newcastle United	W	2-1	Evans 23, Thompson 85

November	2	(a)	West Bromwich Albion	D	0-0	
	9	(h)	Chelsea	W	2-1	Callaghan 25, Smith (pen) 28
	16	(a)	Sheffield Wednesday	W	2-1	Lawler 28, Callaghan 71
	23	(h)	Coventry City	W	2-0	Strong 36, Callaghan 83
	30	(a)	Nottingham Forest	W	1-0	Hunt 24
December	3	(h)	Southampton	W	1-0	Callaghan 14
	7	(h)	West Ham United	W	2-0	Hughes 44, Thompson 47
	14	(a)	Manchester United	L	0-1	
	21	(h)	Tottenham Hotspur	W	1-0	Hughes 70
	26	(h)	Burnley	D	1-1	Lawler 43
January	11	(h)	West Bromwich Albion	W	1-0	Thompson 83
	18	(a)	Chelsea	W	2-1	Hunt 65, Evans 72
February	1	(h)	Sheffield Wednesday	W	1-0	Hunt 65
	15	(h)	Nottingham Forest	L	0-2	
	22	(a)	West Ham United	D	1-1	Hunt 51
March	15	(a)	Sunderland	W	2-0	St John 39, Evans 62
	29	(a)	Queens Park Rangers	W	2-1	Smith (pen) 28, Hunt 78
	31	(h)	Arsenal	D	1-1	Smith (pen) 52
April	12	(a)	Leicester City	W	2-1	Hughes 30, Callaghan 56
	19	(h)	Ipswich Town	W	4-0	Thompson 13, Graham 40, 66, St John 90
	22	(a)	Coventry City	D	0-0	
	28	(h)	Leeds United	D	0-0	
May	12	(a)	Manchester City	L	0-1	
	17	(a)	Newcastle United	D	1-1	Hunt 68

1969/70

August	9	(h)	Chelsea	W	4-1	Lawler 26, St John 49, 83, Strong 60
	12	(h)	Manchester City	W	3-2	St John 2, 88, Hunt 83
	16	(a)	Tottenham Hotspur	W	2-0	Hughes 2, Lawler 37
	20	(a)	Manchester City	W	2-0	Graham 44, 80
	23	(h)	Burnley	D	3-3	Smith (pen) 36, 77, Graham 49
	27	(a)	Crystal Palace	W	3-1	Hughes 36, Hunt 73, Thompson 82
	30	(a)	Sheffield Wednesday	D	1-1	Lawler 42
September	6	(h)	Coventry City	W	2-1	St John 37, Strong 89
	9	(h)	Sunderland	W	2-0	Strong 12, Smith 34
	13	(a)	Manchester United	L	0-1	
	20	(h)	Stoke City	W	3-1	Hunt 15, Hughes 22, Callaghan 64

	27	(a)	West Bromwich Albion	D	2–2	Graham 25, Hunt 89
October	4	(h)	Nottingham Forest	D	1–1	Chapman (og) 50
	7	(h)	Tottenham Hotspur	D	0–0	
	11	(a)	Newcastle United	L	0–1	
	18	(a)	Ipswich Town	D	2–2	Graham 8, Lindsay 76
	25	(h)	Southampton	W	4–1	Hughes 10, Hunt 83, 84, Byrne (og) 88
November	1	(a)	Derby County	L	0–4	
	8	(h)	Wolves	D	0–0	
	15	(h)	West Ham United	W	2–0	Lawler 27, Graham 60
	22	(a)	Leeds United	D	1–1	Yeats 31
	29	(h)	Arsenal	L	0–1	
December	6	(a)	Everton	W	3–0	Hughes 47, Brown (og) 54 Graham 74
	13	(h)	Manchester United	L	1–4	Hughes
	26	(a)	Burnley	W	5–1	Ross 26, Graham 39, Lawler 41, Thompson 52, Callaghan 60
January	10	(a)	Stoke City	W	2–0	Graham 33, Thompson 70
	17	(h)	West Bromwich Albion	D	1–1	Lawler 70
	31	(a)	Nottingham Forest	L	0–1	
February	16	(h)	Newcastle United	D	0–0	
	20	(h)	Derby County	L	0–2	
March	3	(a)	Coventry City	W	3–2	Hughes 38, Evans 65, 72
	7	(h)	Leeds United	D	0–0	
	11	(a)	Southampton	W	1–0	Evans 43
	14	(a)	Arsenal	L	1–2	Yeats
	16	(h)	Sheffield Wednesday	W	3–0	Lawler 50, Yeats 63, Graham 88
	21	(h)	Everton	L	0–2	
	24	(h)	Ipswich Town	W	3–0	Callaghan 32, Smith (pen) 43
	28	(a)	West Ham United	L	0–1	
	30	(a)	Wolves	W	1–0	Lawler 43
April	3	(h)	Crystal Palace	W	3–0	Graham 16, 48, Lawler 47
	15	(a)	Sunderland	W	1–0	Lawler 86

1970/71

August	15	(a)	Burnley	W	2–1	A. Evans 19, Hughes 77
	17	(a)	Blackpool	D	0–0	
	22	(h)	Huddersfield Town	W	4–0	McLaughlin 9, 39, A. Evans 74, 80
	25	(h)	Crystal Palace	D	1–1	Graham 28
	29	(a)	West Bromwich Albion	D	1–1	A. Evans 25

September	5	(h)	Manchester United	D	1-1	A. Evans 22
	12	(a)	Newcastle United	D	0-0	
	19	(h)	Nottingham Forest	W	3-0	Graham 15, Thompson 27, A. Evans 69
	26	(a)	Southampton	L	0-1	
October	3	(h)	Chelsea	W	1-0	A. Evans 22
	10	(a)	Tottenham Hotspur	L	0-1	
	17	(h)	Burnley	W	2-0	Yeats 44, Heighway 51
	24	(a)	Ipswich Town	L	0-1	
	31	(h)	Wolves	W	2-0	Smith (pen) 48, A. Evans 72
November	7	(a)	Derby County	D	0-0	
	14	(h)	Coventry City	D	0-0	
	21	(h)	Everton	W	3-2	Heighway 69, Toshack 76, Lawler 84
	28	(a)	Arsenal	L	0-2	
December	5	(h)	Leeds United	D	1-1	Toshack 52
	12	(a)	West Ham United	W	2-1	Whitham 27, Boersma 43
	19	(a)	Huddersfield Town	D	0-0	
	26	(h)	Stoke City	D	0-0	
January	9	(h)	Blackpool	D	2-2	Heighway 38, Craven (og) 82
	12	(h)	Manchester City	D	0-0	
	16	(a)	Crystal Palace	L	0-1	
	30	(h)	Arsenal	W	2-0	Toshack 4, Smith (pen) 50
February	6	(a)	Leeds United	W	1-0	Toshack 2
	16	(h)	West Ham United	W	1-0	Toshack 58
	20	(a)	Everton	D	0-0	
	27	(a)	Wolves	L	0-1	
March	13	(a)	Coventry City	L	0-1	
	20	(h)	Derby County	W	2-0	Mackay (og) 42, Lawler 80
	29	(h)	Ipswich Town	W	2-0	A. Evans 17, Graham 60
April	2	(h)	West Bromwich Albion	D	1-1	A. Evans 83
	6	(h)	Newcastle United	D	1-1	Lawler 44
	10	(a)	Stoke City	W	1-0	Thompson 32
	17	(h)	Tottenham Hotspur	D	0-0	
	24	(a)	Nottingham Forest	W	1-0	Hall 68
May	1	(h)	Southampton	W	1-0	Hughes 30

1971/72

August	14	(h)	Nottingham Forest	W	3-1	Keegan 12, Smith (pen) 15, Hughes 55
	17	(h)	Wolves	W	3-2	Toshack 7, Heighway 27, Smith (pen) 89
	21	(a)	Newcastle United	L	2-3	Hughes, Keegan
	24	(a)	Crystal Palace	W	1-0	Toshack 57

	28	(h)	Leicester City	W	3-2	Heighway 25, Keegan 35, Toshack 71
September	1	(a)	Manchester City	L	0-1	
	4	(a)	Tottenham Hotspur	L	0-2	
	11	(h)	Southampton	W	1-0	Toshack 32
	18	(a)	Leeds United	L	0-1	
	25	(h)	Manchester United	D	0-0	
October	2	(a)	Stoke City	D	0-0	
	9	(h)	Chelsea	D	0-0	
	16	(a)	Nottingham Forest	W	3-2	Hughes 5, Heighway 55, Smith (pen) 78
	23	(h)	Huddersfield Town	W	2-0	Smith (pen) 57, Evans 80
	30	(a)	Sheffield United	D	1-1	Keegan 47
November	6	(h)	Arsenal	W	3-2	Hughes 41, Callaghan 55, Ross 87
	13	(a)	Everton	L	0-1	
	20	(a)	Coventry City	W	2-0	Whitham 80, 89
	27	(h)	West Ham United	W	1-0	Hughes 69
December	4	(a)	Ipswich Town	D	0-0	
	11	(h)	Derby County	W	3-2	Whitham 14, 44, 53
	18	(h)	Tottenham Hotspur	D	0-0	
	27	(a)	West Bromwich Albion	L	0-1	
January	1	(h)	Leeds United	L	0-2	
	8	(a)	Leicester City	L	0-1	
	22	(a)	Wolves	D	0-0	
	29	(h)	Crystal Palace	W	4-1	Lawler 38, 66, Callaghan 72, Keegan 82
February	12	(a)	Huddersfield Town	W	1-0	Whitham 71
	19	(h)	Sheffield United	W	2-0	Toshack 42, 82
	26	(h)	Manchester City	W	3-0	Lloyd 37, Keegan 53, Graham 65
March	4	(h)	Everton	W	4-0	Wright (og) 1, McLaughlin(og) 66, Lawler 74, Hughes 87
	11	(a)	Chelsea	D	0-0	
	18	(h)	Newcastle United	W	5-0	Lawler 5, Keegan 22, Toshack 39, Hughes 63, Heighway 81
	25	(a)	Southampton	W	1-0	Toshack 52
	28	(h)	Stoke City	W	2-1	Burrows (og) 40, Keegan 53
April	1	(h)	West Bromwich Albion	W	2-0	Smith (pen) 1, Lawler 58
	3	(a)	Manchester United	W	3-0	Lawler 60, Toshack 62, Hughes 84
	8	(H)	Coventry City	W	3-1	Keegan 21, Smith (pen) 67, Toshack 85
	15	(a)	West Ham United	W	2-0	Toshack 9, Heighway 46

	22	(h)	Ipswich Town	W	2–0	Toshack 39, 66
May	1	(a)	Derby County	L	0–1	
	8	(a)	Arsenal	D	0–0	

1972/73

August	12	(h)	Manchester City	W	2–0	Hall 3, Callaghan 84
	15	(h)	Manchester United	W	2–0	Toshack 12, Heighway 20
	19	(a)	Crystal Palace	D	1–1	Hughes 75
	23	(a)	Chelsea	W	2–1	Toshack 3, Callaghan 13
	30	(a)	Leicester City	L	2–3	Toshack 1, 16
September	2	(a)	Derby County	L	1–2	Toshack 16
	9	(h)	Wolves	W	4–2	Hughes 20, Cormack 76, Smith (pen) 80, Keegan 84
	16	(a)	Arsenal	D	0–0	
	23	(h)	Sheffield United	W	5–0	Boersma 28, Lindsay 31, Heighway 33, Cormack 51, Keegan (pen) 54
	30	(a)	Leeds United	W	2–1	Lloyd 40, Boersma 65
October	7	(h)	Everton	W	1–0	Cormack 77
	14	(a)	Southampton	D	1–1	Lawler 40
	21	(h)	Stoke City	W	2–1	Hughes 66, Callaghan 90
November	4	(h)	Chelsea	W	3–1	Toshack 33, 55, Keegan 50
	11	(a)	Manchester United	L	0–2	
	18	(h)	Newcastle United	W	3–2	Cormack 5, Lindsay 35, Toshack 48
	25	(a)	Tottenham Hotspur	W	2–1	Heighway 28, Keegan 40
December	2	(h)	Birmingham City	W	4–3	Lindsay 32, 55, Cormack 44, Toshack 77
	9	(a)	West Bromwich Albion	D	1–1	Boersma 21
	16	(a)	Ipswich Town	D	1–1	Heighway 24
	23	(h)	Coventry City	W	2–0	Toshack 6, 22
	26	(a)	Sheffield United	W	3–0	Beorsma 27, Lawler 50, Heighway 81
	30	(h)	Crystal Palace	W	1–0	Cormack 66
January	6	(a)	West Ham United	W	1–0	Keegan 75
	20	(h)	Derby County	D	1–1	Toshack 23
	27	(a)	Wolves	L	1–2	Keegan 17
February	10	(h)	Arsenal	L	0–2	
	17	(a)	Manchester City	D	1–1	Boersma 77
	24	(h)	Ipswich Town	W	2–1	Heighway 67, Keegan 80
March	3	(a)	Everton	W	2–0	Hughes 80, 88
	10	(h)	Southampton	W	3–2	Lloyd 37, Keegan 38, 87
	17	(a)	Stoke City	W	1–0	Mahoney (og) 65
	24	(h)	Norwich City	W	3–1	Lawler 50, Hughes 55, Hall 88

	31	(h)	Tottenham Hotspur	D	1-1	Keegan 70
April	7	(a)	Birmingham City	L	1-2	Smith 60
	14	(h)	West Bromwich Albion	W	1-0	Keegan (pen) 14
	17	(a)	Coventry City	W	2-1	Boersma 36, 60
	21	(a)	Newcastle United	L	1-2	Keegan 24
	23	(h)	Leeds United	W	2-0	Cormack 47, Keegan 85
	28	(h)	Leicester City	D	0-0	

1973/74

September	25	(h)	Stoke City	W	1-0	Heighway 6
August	25	(h)	Stoke City	W	1-0	Heighway 6
	28	(a)	Coventry City	L	0-1	
September	1	(a)	Leicester City	D	1-1	Toshack 50
	4	(h)	Derby County	W	2-0	Thompson 35, Keegan (pen) 85
	8	(h)	Chelsea	W	1-0	Keegan 35
	12	(a)	Derby County	L	1-3	Boersma 26
	15	(a)	Birmingham City	D	1-1	Hall 85
	22	(h)	Tottenham Hotspur	W	3-2	Lawler 28, 90, Lindsay (pen) 76
	29	(a)	Manchester United	D	0-0	
October	6	(h)	Newcastle United	W	2-1	Cormack 20, Lindsay (pen) 86
	13	(a)	Southampton	L	0-1	
	20	(a)	Leeds United	L	0-1	
	27	(h)	Sheffield United	W	1-0	Keegan 26
November	3	(a)	Arsenal	W	2-0	Hughes 77, Toshack 65
	10	(h)	Wolves	W	1-0	Heighway 22
	17	(h)	Ipswich Town	W	4-2	Keegan 17, 22 (pen), 90, Cormack 44
	24	(a)	Queens Park Rangers	D	2-2	Lloyd 26, Toshack 75
December	1	(h)	West Ham United	W	1-0	Cormack 14
	8	(a)	Everton	W	1-0	Waddle 67
	15	(a)	Norwich City	D	1-1	Cormack 17
	22	(h)	Manchester United	W	2-0	Keegan (pen) 30, Heighway 65
	26	(a)	Barnsley	L	1-2	Cormack 84
	29	(a)	Chelsea	W	1-0	Cormack 21
January	1	(h)	Leicester City	D	1-1	Cormack 67
	12	(h)	Birmingham City	W	3-2	Keegan 15, 31, Thompson 69
	19	(a)	Stoke City	D	1-1	Smith 90
February	2	(h)	Norwich City	W	1-0	Cormack 90
	5	(h)	Coventry City	W	2-1	Lindsay (pen) 28, Keegan 57
	23	(a)	Newcastle United	D	0-0	
	26	(h)	Southampton	W	1-0	Boersma 87

March	2	(h)	Burnley	W	1-0	Toshack 89
	16	(h)	Leeds United	W	1-0	Heighway 82
	23	(a)	Wolves	W	1-0	Hall 27
April	6	(h)	Queens Park Rangers	W	2-0)	Lindsay (pen) 7, Mancini (og) 29
	8	(a)	Sheffield United	L	0-1	
	12	(a)	Manchester City	D	1-1	Cormack 18
	13	(a)	Ipswich Town	D	1-1	Hughes 62
	16	(h)	Manchester City	W	4-0	Hall 3, 12, Boersma 16, Keegan 35
	20	(h)	Everton	D	0-0	
	24	(h)	Arsenal	L	0-1	
	27	(a)	West Ham United	D	2-2	Toshack 58, Keegan 90
May	8	(a)	Tottenham Hotspur	D	1-1	Heighway 67

1974/75

August	17	(a)	Luton Town	W	2-1	Smith 31, Heighway 74
	20	(a)	Wolves	D	0-0	
	24	(h)	Leicester City	W	2-1	Lindsay 1, 64 (both pens)
	27	(h)	Wolves	W	2-0	Heighway 51, Toshack 56
	31	(a)	Chelsea	W	3-0	Kennedy 22, Boersma 54, 76
September	7	(h)	Tottenham Hotspur	W	5-2	Boersma 4, 9, 41, Hughes 71, Kennedy 87
	14	(a)	Manchester City	L	0-2	
	21	(h)	Stoke City	W	3-0	Richie (og) 43, Boersma 45, Heighway 55
	24	(h)	Burnley	L	0-1	
	28	(a)	Sheffield United	L	0-1	
October	5	(a)	Carlisle United	W	1-0	Kennedy 36
	12	(h)	Middlesbrough	W	2-0	Callaghan 52, Keegan (pen) 83
	19	(a)	Queens Park Rangers	W	1-0	Hall 6
	26	(h)	Leeds United	W	1-0	Heighway 73
November	2	(a)	Ipswich Town	L	0-1	
	9	(h)	Arsenal	L	1-3	Kennedy 53
	16	(a)	Everton	D	0-0	
	23	(h)	West Ham United	D	1-1	Smith 12
	30	(a)	Coventry City	D	1-1	Keegan 48
December	7	(h)	Derby County	D	2-2	Kennedy 18, Heighway 22
	14	(h)	Luton Town	W	2-0	Toshack 46, Heighway 85
	21	(a)	Birmingham City	L	1-3	Toshack 43
	26	(h)	Manchester City	W	4-1	Hall 22, 72, Toshack 25, Heighway 41

January	11	(a)	Derby County	L	0–2	
	18	(h)	Coventry City	W	2–1	Heighway 35, Keegan 89
February	1	(a)	Arsenal	L	0–2	
	8	(h)	Ipswich Town	W	5–2	Hall 6, Toshack 9, 65, Lindsay 42, Cormack 87
	12	(a)	Newcastle United	L	1–4	Hall 61
	19	(a)	West Ham United	D	0–0	
	22	(h)	Everton	D	0–0	
March	1	(h)	Chelsea	D	2–2	Heighway 40, Cormack 89
	8	(a)	Burnley	D	1–1	McDermott 74
	15	(h)	Sheffield United	D	0–0	
	19	(a)	Leicester City	D	1–1	Toshack 35
	22	(a)	Tottenham Hotspur	W	2–0	Keegan 46, Cormack 66
	25	(h)	Newcastle United	W	4–0	Keegan 7, Toshack 43, 70, McDermott 72
	29	(h)	Birmingham City	W	1–0	Keegan (pen) 64
	31	(a)	Stoke City	L	0–2	
April	5	(a)	Leeds United	W	2–0	Keegan 41, 51
	12	(h)	Carlisle United	W	2–0	Toshack 64, Keegan 74
	19	(a)	Middlesbrough	L	0–1	
	26	(h)	Queens Park Rangers	W	3–1	Toshack 16, 85, Keegan (pen) 52

1975/76

August	16	(a)	Queens Park Rangers	L	0–2	
	19	(h)	West Ham United	D	2–2	Callaghan 24, Toshack 81
	23	(h)	Tottenham Hotspur	W	3–2	Keegan (pen) 54, Case 60, Heighway 72
	26	(a)	Leeds United	W	3–0	Kennedy 26, Callaghan 84, 88
	30	(a)	Leicester City	D	1–1	Keegan 50
September	6	(h)	Sheffield United	W	1–0	Kennedy 70
	13	(a)	Ipswich Town	L	0–2	
	20	(h)	Aston Villa	W	3–0	Toshack 62, Keegan 77, Case 86
	27	(a)	Everton	D	0–0	
October	4	(h)	Wolves	W	2–0	Hall 60, Case 86
	11	(h)	Birmingham City	W	3–1	Toshack 13, 59, 86
	18	(a)	Coventry City	D	0–0	
	25	(h)	Derby County	D	1–1	Toshack 27
November	8	(h)	Manchester United	W	3–1	Heighway 12, Toshack 46, Keegan 78
	15	(a)	Newcastle United	W	2–1	Hall 4, Kennedy 88
	22	(h)	Coventry City	D	1–1	Toshack 28
	29	(h)	Norwich City	L	1–3	Hughes 87

December	2	(h)	Arsenal	D	2-2	Neal 23, 59 (both pens)
	6	(a)	Burnley	D	0-0	
	13	(a)	Tottenham Hotspur	W	4-0	Keegan 43, Case 54, Neal 74, Heighway 86
	20	(h)	Queens Park Rangers	W	2-0	Toshack 22, Neal (pen) 75
	26	(a)	Stoke City	D	1-1	Toshack 8
	27	(h)	Manchester City	W	1-0	Cormack 61
January	10	(h)	Ipswich Town	W	3-3	Keegan 13, 33, Case 78
	17	(a)	Sheffield United	D	0-0	
	31	(a)	West Ham United	W	4-0	Toshack 63, 75, 81, Keegan 88
February	7	(h)	Leeds United	W	2-0	Keegan 40, Toshack 71
	18	(a)	Manchester United	D	0-0	
	21	(h)	Newcastle United	W	2-0	Keegan 26, Case 51
	24	(a)	Arsenal	L	0-1	
	28	(a)	Derby County	D	1-1	Kennedy 86
March	6	(h)	Middlesbrough	L	0-2	
	13	(a)	Birmingham City	W	1-0	Neal (pen) 83
	20	(a)	Norwich City	W	1-0	Fairclough 59
	27	(h)	Burnley	W	2-0	Fairclough 39, 61
April	3	(h)	Everton	W	1-0	Fairclough 88
	6	(h)	Leicester City	W	1-0	Keegan 58
	10	(a)	Aston Villa	D	0-0	
	17	(h)	Stoke City	W	5-3	Neal (pen) 37, Toshack 43, Kennedy 51, Hughes 73, Fairclough 78
	19	(a)	Manchester City	W	3-0	Heighway 73, Fairclough 88, 89
May	4	(a)	Wolves	W	3-1	Keegan 76, Toshack 85, Kennedy 89

1976/77

August	21	(h)	Norwich City	W	1-0	Heighway 55
	25	(a)	West Bromwich Albion	W	1-0	Toshack 40
	28	(a)	Birmingham City	L	1-2	Johnson 75
September	4	(h)	Coventry City	W	3-1	Keegan 56, Johnson 73, Toshack 80
	11	(a)	Derby County	W	3-2	Kennedy 6, Toshack 54, Keegan 80
	18	(h)	Tottenham Hotspur	W	2-0	Johnson 7, Heighway 30
	25	(a)	Newcastle United	L	0-1	
October	2	(h)	Middlesbrough	D	0-0	
	16	(h)	Everton	W	3-1	Heighway 7, Neil (pen) 12, Toshack 41
	23	(a)	Leeds United	D	1-1	Kennedy 72

	27	(a)	Leicester City	W	1-0	Toshack 12
	30	(h)	Aston Villa	W	3-0	Callaghan 76, McDermott 80, Keegan 86
November	6	(a)	Sunderland	W	1-0	Fairclough 76
	9	(h)	Leicester City	W	5-1	Heighway 26, Toshack 32, Neal (pen) 70, Jones 72, Keegan (pen) 82
	20	(a)	Arsenal	D	1-1	Kennedy 88
	27	(h)	Bristol City	W	2-1	Keegan 44, Jones 56
December	4	(a)	Ipswich Town	L	0-1	
	11	(h)	Queens Park Rangers	W	3-1	Toshack 34, Keegan 84, Kennedy 85
	15	(a)	Aston Villa	L	1-5	Kennedy 41
	18	(a)	West Ham United	L	0-2	
	27	(h)	Stoke City	W	4-0	Thompson 5, Neal (pen) 62, Keegan 67, Johnson 81
	29	(a)	Manchester City	D	1-1	Watson (og) 89
January	1	(h)	Sunderland	W	2-0	Kennedy 13, Thompson 69
	15	(h)	West Bromwich Albion	D	1-1	Fairclough 84
	22	(a)	Norwich City	L	1-2	Neal (pen) 52
February	5	(h)	Birmingham City	W	4-1	Neal (pen) 37, Toshack 42, 72, Heighway 79
	16	(a)	Manchester United	D	0-0	
	19	(h)	Derby County	W	3-1	Toshack 56, Jones 69, Keegan 84
March	5	(h)	Newcastle United	W	1-0	Heighway 11
	9	(a)	Tottenham Hotspur	L	0-1	
	12	(a)	Middlesbrough	W	1-0	Hughes 41
	22	(a)	Everton	D	0-0	
April	2	(h)	Leeds United	W	3-1	Neal (pen) 36, Fairclough 38, Heighway 61
	9	(h)	Manchester City	W	2-1	Keegan 43, Heighway 78
	11	(a)	Stoke City	D	0-0	
	16	(h)	Arsenal	W	2-0	Neal 20, Keegan 77
	30	(h)	Ipswich Town	W	2-1	Kennedy 70, Keegan 73
May	3	(h)	Manchester United	W	1-0	Keegan 15
	7	(a)	Queens Park Rangers	D	1-1	Case 68
	10	(a)	Coventry City	D	0-0	
	14	(h)	West Ham United	D	0-0	
	16	(a)	Bristol City	L	1-2	Johnson 30

1977/78

August	20	(a) Middlesbrough	D	1-1	Dalglish 7
	23	(h) Newcastle United	W	2-0	Dalglish 46, McDermott 87
	27	(h) West Bromwich Albion	W	3-0	Dalglish 18, Heighway 81, Case 85
September	3	(a) Birmingham City	W	1-0	R. Kennedy 2
	10	(h) Coventry City	W	2-0	Fairclough 65, Dalglish 67
	17	(a) Ipswich Town	D	1-1	Dalglish 22
October	8	(h) Chelsea	W	2-0	Dalglish 2, Fairclough 79
	15	(a) Leeds United	W	2-1	Case 36, 63
	22	(h) Everton	D	0-0	
	29	(a) Manchester City	L	1-3	Fairclough
November	5	(h) Aston Villa	L	1-2	Carrodus (og) 65
	12	(a) Queens Park Rangers	L	0-2	
	19	(h) Bristol City	D	1-1	Dalglish 12
	26	(a) Leicester City	W	4-0	Fairclough 18, Heighway 69, Dalglish 81, McDermott 84
December	3	(h) West Ham United	W	2-0	Dalglish 37, Fairclough 82
	10	(a) Norwich City	L	1-2	Thompson 80
	17	(h) Queens Park Rangers	W	1-0	Neal (pen) 30
	26	(a) Nottingham Forest	D	1-1	Heighway 30
	27	(h) Wolves	W	1-0	Neal (pen) 22
	31	(a) Newcastle United	W	2-0	Thompson 48, Dalglish 89
January	2	(h) Middlesbrough	W	2-0	Johnson 39, Heighway 80
	14	(a) West Bromwich Albion	W	1-0	Johnson 10
	21	(h) Birmingham City	L	2-3	Thompson 74, R. Kennedy 87
February	4	(a) Coventry City	L	0-1	
	25	(h) Manchester United	W	3-1	Souness 39, R. Kennedy 49, Case 84
March	4	(a) Chelsea	L	1-3	Neal (pen) 38
	8	(a) Derby County	L	2-4	Fairclough 70, Dalglish 88
	11	(h) Leeds United	W	1-0	Dalglish 47
	25	(a) Wolves	W	3-1	Case 35, Dalglish 73, 82
April	1	(a) Aston Villa	W	3-0	Dalglish 3, 19, Kennedy 21
	5	(a) Everton	W	1-0	Johnson 13
	8	(h) Leicester City	W	3-2	Smith 42, 76, Lee 56
	15	(a) Bristol City	D	1-1	Heighway 41

	18	(h)	Ipswich Town	D	2–2	Dalglish 58, Souness 62
	22	(h)	Norwich City	W	3–0	Ryan (og) 4, Fairclough 35, 46
	25	(h)	Arsenal	W	1–0	Fairclough 24
	29	(a)	West Ham United	W	2–0	McDermott 38, Fairclough 66
May	1	(h)	Manchester City	W	4–0	Dalglish 24, 55, 80, Neal (pen) 53
	4		Nottingham Forest	D	0–0	

1978/79

August	19	(h)	Queens Park Rangers	W	2–1	Dalglish 27, Heighway 76
	22	(a)	Ipswich Town	W	3–0	Souness 17, Dalglish 22, 74
	26	(a)	Manchester City	W	4–1	Souness 15, 48, R. Kennedy 34, Dalglish 56
September	2	(h)	Tottenham Hotspur	W	7–0	Dalglish 8, 20, R. Kennedy 28, Johnson 48, 58, Neal (pen) 64, McDermott 76
	16	(h)	Coventry City	W	1–0	Souness 27
	23	(a)	West Bromwich Albion	D	1–1	Dalglish 70
December	26	(a)	Manchester United	W	3–0	R. Kennedy 5, Case 25, Fairclough 67
February	3	(h)	West Bromwich Albion	W	2–1	Dalglish 21, Fairclough 53
	13	(h)	Birmingham City	W	1–0	Souness 37
	21	(h)	Norwich City	W	6–0	Dalglish 3, 48, Johnson 46, 51, A. Kennedy 80, R. Kennedy 90
	24	(a)	Derby County	W	2–0	Dalglish 11, R. Kennedy 70
March	3	(a)	Chelsea	D	0–0	
	6	(a)	Coventry City	D	0–0	
	13	(h)	Everton	D	1–1	Dalglish 15
	20	(h)	Wolves	W	2–0	McDermott 34, Johnson 48
	24	(h)	Ipswich Town	W	2–0	Dalglish 41, Johnson 81

FA CUP 1967/68

January	27	(a)	Bournemouth	D	0–0
	30	(h)	Bournemouth	W	4–1
February	17	(a)	Walsall	D	0–0
	19	(h)	Walsall	W	5–2
March	9	(a)	Tottenham Hotspur	D	1–1
	12	(h)	Tottenham Hotspur	W	2–1
	30	(a)	West Bromwich Albion	D	0–0
April	8	(h)	West Bromwich Albion	D	1–1*
	18		West Bromwich Albion	L	1–2**

*After extra time
**played at Maine Road

1968/69

January	4	(h)	Doncaster Rovers	W	3–0
	25	(h)	Burnley	W	2–1
March	1	(a)	Leicester City	D	0–0
	3	(h)	Leicester City	L	0–1

1969/70

January	7	(a)	Coventry City	D	1–1
	12	(h)	Coventry City	W	3–0
	24	(h)	Wrexham	W	3–1
February	7	(h)	Leicester City	D	0–0
	11	(a)	Leicester City	W	3–0
	21	(a)	Watford	L	0–1

1970/71

January	2	(h)	Aldershot	W	1–0
	23	(h)	Swansea City	W	3–0
February	13	(h)	Southampton	W	1–0
March	6	(h)	Tottenham Hotspur	D	0–0
	16	(a)	Tottenham Hotspur	W	1–0
	27		Everton	W	2–1*
May	8		Arsenal	L	1–2**

*Played at Old Trafford
**After extra time

1971/72

January	15	(a)	Oxford United	W	3–0
February	5	(h)	Leeds United	D	0–0
	9	(a)	Leeds United	L	0–2

1972/73

January	13	(a)	Burnley	D	0–0
	16	(h)	Burnley	W	3–0
February	4	(h)	Manchester City	D	0–0
	7	(a)	Manchester City	L	0–2

1973/74

January	5	(h)	Doncaster Rovers	D	2–2
	8	(a)	Doncaster Rovers	W	2–0
	26	(h)	Carlisle United	D	0–0
	29	(a)	Carlisle United	W	2–0
February	16	(h)	Ipswich Town	W	2–0
March	9	(a)	Bristol City	W	1–0
	30		Leicester City	D	0–0★
April	3		Leicester City	D	3–1★★
May	4		Newcastle United	W	3–0

★Played at Old Trafford
★★Played at Villa Park

1974/75

January	4	(h)	Stoke City	W	3–0
	25	(a)	Ipswich Town	L	0–1

1975/76

January	3	(a)	West Ham United	W	2–0
	24	(a)	Derby County	L	0–1

1976/77

January	8	(h)	Crystal Palace	D	0-0
	11	(a)	Crystal Palace	W	3-2
	29	(h)	Carlisle United	W	3-0
February	26	(h)	Oldham Athletic	W	3-1
March	19	(h)	Middlesbrough	W	2-0
April	23		Everton	D	2-2★
	27		Everton	W	3-0★★
May	21		Manchester United	L	1-2

★ Played at Maine Road
★★ Played at Maine Road

1977/78

January	7	(a)	Chelsea	L	2-4

1978/79

January	10	(a)	Southend United	D	0-0
	17	(h)	Southend United	W	3-0
	30	(h)	Blackburn Rovers	W	1-0
February	28	(h)	Burnley	W	1-0
March	10	(a)	Ipswich Town	W	1-0
	31		Manchester United	D	2-2★
April	4		Manchester United	L	0-1★★

★ Played at Maine Road
★★ Played at Goodison Park

LEAGUE CUP 1967/68

September	13	(h)	Bolton Wanderers	D	1-1
	27	(a)	Bolton Wanderers	L	2-3

1968/69

September	4	(h)	Sheffield United	W	4-0
	25	(h)	Swansea Town	W	2-0
October	15	(a)	Arsenal	L	1-0

1969/70

September	3	(a)	Watford	W	2–1
	24	(a)	Manchester City	L	2–3

1970/71

September	8	(a)	Mansfield Town	D	0–0
	22	(h)	Mansfield Town	W	3–2★
October	6	(a)	Swindon Town	L	0–2

★ After extra time

1971/72

September	9	(h)	Hull City	W	3–0
October	5	(h)	Southampton	W	1–0
	27	(a)	West Ham United	L	1–2

1972/73

September	5	(a)	Carlisle United	D	1–1
	19	(h)	Carlisle United	W	5–1
October	3	(a)	West Bromwich Albion	D	1–1
	10	(h)	West Bromwich Albion	W	2–1★
	31	(h)	Leeds United	D	2–2
November	22	(a)	Leeds United	W	1–0
December	4	(h)	Tottenham Hotspur	D	1–1
	6	(a)	Tottenham Hotspur	L	1–3

★ After extra time

1973/74

October	8	(a)	West Ham United	D	2–2
	29	(h)	West Ham United	W	1–0
November	21	(a)	Sunderland	W	2–0
	27	(a)	Hull City	D	0–0
December	4	(h)	Hull City	W	3–1
	19	(a)	Wolves	L	0–1

1974/75

September	10	(h)	Brentford	W	2-1
October	8	(a)	Bristol City	D	0-0
	16	(h)	Bristol City	W	4-0
November	12	(h)	Middlesbrough	L	0-1

1975/76

September	10	(a)	York City	W	1-0
October	7	(h)	Barnsley	D	1-1
	14	(a)	Barnsley	L	0-1

1976/77

August	31	(h)	West Bromwich Albion	D	1-1
September	6	(a)	West Bromwich Albion	L	0-1

1977/78

August	30	(h)	Chelsea	W	2-0
October	26	(h)	Derby County	W	2-0
November	29	(h)	Coventry City	D	2-2
December	20	(a)	Coventry City	W	2-0
January	17	(a)	Wrexham	W	3-1
February	7	(h)	Arsenal	W	2-1
	14	(a)	Arsenal	D	0-0
March	18		Nottingham Forest	D	0-0*
	22		Nottingham Forest	L	0-1**

★ Played at Wembley. After extra time
★★ Played at Old Trafford

1978/79

August	28	(a)	Sheffield United	L	0-1

EUROPEAN CUP 1973/74

First round

| September 10 | v. | Jeunesse D'Esch | (a) | 1-1 |
| October 3 | v. | Jeunesse D'Esch | (h) | 2-0 |

Second round

| October 24 | v. | Red Star Belgrade | (a) | 1-2 |
| November 6 | v. | Red Star Belgrade | (h) | 1-2 |

1976/77

First round

| September 14 | v. | Crusaders | (h) | 2-0 |
| September 28 | v. | Crusaders | (a) | 5-0 |

Second round

| October 20 | v. | Trabzonspor | (a) | 0-1 |
| November 3 | v. | Trabzonspor | (h) | 3-0 |

Quarter-final

| March 2 | v. | AS St Etienne | (a) | 0-1 |
| March 16 | v. | AS St Etienne | (h) | 3-1 |

Semi-final

| April 6 | v. | FC Zurich | (a) | 3-1 |
| April 20 | v. | FC Zurich | (h) | 3-0 |

Final

| May 25 | v. | Borussia Moenchengladbach | | 3-1★ |

★Played in Rome

1977/78

Second round

| October 19 | v. | SG Dynamo Dresden | (h) | 5-1 |
| November 2 | v. | SG Dynamo Dresden | (a) | 1-2 |

Quarter-final

| March 1 | v. | Benfica | (a) | 2-1 |
| March 15 | v. | Benfica | (h) | 4-1 |

Semi-final

| March 29 | v. | Borussia Moenchengladbach | (a) | 1-2 |
| April 12 | v. | Borussia Moenchengladbach | (h) | 3-0 |

Final

| May 10 | v. | Club Bruges | | 1-0* |

*Played at Wembley

1978/79

First round

| September 13 | v. | Nottingham Forest | (a) | 0-2 |
| September 27 | v. | Nottingham Forest | (h) | 0-0 |

EUROPEAN FAIRS CUP 1967/68

First round

| September 19 | v. | Malmö | (a) | 2-0 |
| October 4 | v. | Malmö | (h) | 2-1 |

Second round

| November 7 | v. | TSV Munich 1860 | (h) | 8-0 |
| November 14 | v. | TSV Munich 1860 | (a) | 1-2 |

Third round

| November 28 | v. | Ferencvaros | (a) | 0-1 |
| January 9 | v. | Ferencvaros | (h) | 0-1 |

1968/69

First round

| September 18 | v. | Athletic Bilbao | (h) | 1-2 |
| October 2 | v. | Athletic Bilbao | (h) | 2-1* |

*After extra time (Liverpool lost on the toss of a coin)

1969/70

First round

| September 16 | v. | Dundalk | (h) | 10-0 |
| September 30 | v. | Dundalk | (a) | 4-0 |

Second round
| November 12 | v. | Vitoria Setubal | (a) | 0-1 |
| November 26 | v. | Vitoria Setubal | (h) | 3-2 |

1970/71

First round
| September 15 | v. | Ferencvaros | (h) | 1-0 |
| September 29 | v. | Ferencvaros | (a) | 1-1 |

Second round
| October 21 | v. | Dinamo Bucharest | (h) | 3-0 |
| November 4 | v. | Dinamo Bucharest | (a) | 1-1 |

Third round
December 9	v.	Hibernian	(a)	1-0
December 22	v.	Hibernian	(h)	2-0
March 3	v.	Bayern Munich	(h)	3-0
March 24	v.	Bayern Munich	(a)	1-1
April 14	v.	Leeds United	(h)	0-1
April 28	v.	Leeds United	(a)	0-0

EUROPEAN CUP-WINNERS' CUP 1971/72

September 15	v.	Servette Geneva	(a)	1-2
September 29	v.	Servette Geneva	(h)	2-0
October 20	v.	Bayern Munich	(a)	1-3

1974/75

September 17	v.	Stromgodset Drammen	(h)	11-0
October 1	v.	Stromgodset Drammen	(a)	1-0
October 23	v.	Ferencvaros	(h)	1-1
November 5	v.	Ferencvaros	(a)	0-0*

* (Liverpool lost on away goals rule)

UEFA CUP 1972/73

Round 1
| September 12 | v. | Eintracht Frankfurt | (h) | 2-0 |
| September 26 | v. | Eintracht Frankfurt | (a) | 0-0 |

Second round
| October 24 | v. | AEK Athens | (h) | 2-0 |
| November 7 | v. | AEK Athens | (a) | 3-1 |

Third round
| November 29 | v. | BFC Dynamo (Berlin) | (a) | 0-0 |
| December 13 | v. | BFC Dynamo (Berlin) | (h) | 3-1 |

Quarter-final
| March 7 | v. | SG Dynamo Dresden | (h) | 2-0 |
| March 21 | v. | SG Dynamo Dresden | (a) | 1-0 |

Semi-final
| April 10 | v. | Tottenham Hotspur | (h) | 1-0 |
| April 25 | v. | Tottenham Hotspur | (a) | 1-2★ |

Final
| May 23 | v. | Borussia Moenchengladbach | (h) | 3-0 |

★ (Liverpool won on away goals rule)

1975/76

First round
| September 17 | v. | Hibernian | (a) | 0-1 |
| September 30 | v. | Hibernian | (h) | 3-1 |

Second round
| October 22 | v. | Real Sociedad | (a) | 3-1 |
| November 4 | v. | Real Sociedad | (h) | 6-0 |

Third round
| November 26 | v. | Slask Wroclaw | (a) | 2-1 |
| December 10 | v. | Slask Wroclaw | (h) | 3-0 |

Quarter-final
| March 3 | v. | SG Dynamo Dresden | (a) | 0-0 |
| March 17 | v. | SG Dynamo Dresden | (h) | 2-1 |

Semi-final
| March 30 | v. | Barcelona | (a) | 1-0 |
| April 14 | v. | Barcelona | (h) | 1-1 |

Final
| April 28 | v. | Club Brugge | (h) | 3-2 |

EUROPEAN SUPER CUP

1977

November 22	v.	Hamburg	(a)	1–1
December 6	v.	Hamburg	(h)	6–0

1978

December 4	v.	Anderlecht	(a)	1–3
December 19	v.	Anderlecht	(h)	2–1

FA CHARITY SHIELD

1971	v.	Leicester City	0–1
1974	v.	Leeds United	1–1★
1976	v.	Southampton	1–0
1977	v.	Manchester United	0–0

★ (Liverpool won 6–5 penalties)

EMLYN HUGHES' ENGLAND RECORD

1969

November 5	v.	Holland	1–0
December 10	v.	Portugal	1–0

1970

February 25	v.	Belgium	3–1
April 18	v.	Wales	1–1
April 21	v.	Northern Ireland	3–1
April 25	v.	Scotland	0–0
November 25	v.	East Germany	3–1

1971

February 3	v.	Malta	1-0
April 21	v.	Greece	3-0
May 12	v.	Malta	5-0
May 19	v.	Wales	0-0
November 10	v.	Switzerland	1-1
December 1	v.	Greece	2-0

1972

April 29	v.	West Germany	1-3
May 13	v.	West Germany	0-0
May 20	v.	Wales	3-0
May 23	v.	Northern Ireland	0-1
May 27	v.	Scotland	1-0
November 15	v.	Wales	1-0

1973

January 24	v.	Wales	1-1
February 14	v.	Scotland	5-0
May 15	v.	Wales	3-0
May 19	v.	Scotland	1-0
June 6	v.	Poland	0-2
June 10	v.	USSR	2-1
June 14	v.	Italy	0-2
September 26	v.	Austria	7-0
October 17	v.	Poland	1-1
November 14	v.	Italy	0-1

1974

May 11	v.	Wales	2-0
May 15	v.	Northern Ireland	1-0
May 18	v.	Scotland	0-2
May 22	v.	Argentina	2-2
May 29	v.	East Germany	1-1
June 1	v.	Bulgaria	1-0
June 5	v.	Yugoslavia	2-2
October 30	v.	Czechoslovakia	3-0
November 20	v.	Portugal	0-0

1975

| May 11 | v. | Cyprus | 1–0 |
| May 17 | v. | Northern Ireland | 0–0 |

1976

| November 17 | v. | Italy | 0–2 |

1977

March 30	v.	Luxembourg	5–0
May 31	v.	Wales	0–1
June 4	v.	Scotland	1–2
June 8	v.	Brazil	0–0
June 12	v.	Argentina	1–1
June 15	v.	Uruguay	0–0
September 7	v.	Switzerland	0–0
October 12	v.	Luxembourg	2–0
November 16	v.	Italy	2–0

1978

February 22	v.	West Germany	1–2
May 16	v.	Northern Ireland	1–0
May 20	v.	Scotland	1–0
May 24	v.	Hungary	4–1
September 20	v.	Denmark	4–3
October 25	v.	Eire	1–1

1979

February 7	v.	Northern Ireland	4–0
May 23	v.	Wales	0–0
June 10	v.	Sweden	0–0

1980

March 26	v.	Spain	2–0
May 20	v.	Northern Ireland	1–1
May 24	v.	Scotland	2–0

MEDALS

European Cup	1976/77
	1977/78
UEFA Cup	1972/73
	1975/76
European Super Cup	1977
League Championship	1972/73
	1975/76
	1976/77
	1978/79
FA Cup	1973/74
Football League Cup	1979/80 (With Wolves)
Football Writers' Footballer of the Year Award	1977

62 England caps
8 England Under-23 caps
4 appearances for the Football League

In the 1972/73 season Emlyn Hughes created a record that still stands. He made 74 appearances in one season: 41 in the League, 4 in the FA Cup, 8 in the League Cup, 12 in the UEFA Cup and 8 international appearances for England. He also played in the Common Market Entry Match at Wembley. Hughes was in the team named 'The Three'. The opposition were known as 'The Six'.

EMLYN HUGHES' RECORD WITH OTHER CLUBS

Blackpool	1965/66	1966/67	27 appearances
Wolverhampton Wanderers	1979/80	1980/81	58 appearances
			2 goals
Rotherham United (player-manager)	1981/82	1982/83	56 appearances
			6 goals
Hull City	1982/83		9 appearances 0 goals
Swansea City	1983/84		7 appearances 0 goals
Mansfield Town	1983/84		0 appearances

BIBLIOGRAPHY

The Saint: My Autobiography, Ian St John, Hodder & Stoughton 2005

Jack & Bobby – A Story of Brothers in Conflict, Leo McKinstry, Collins Willow 2002

A Matter of Opinion, Alan Hansen, Partridge Press 1999

Right Back to the Beginning: the Autobiography, Jimmy Armfield, Headline 2004

My Colourful Life From Red to Amber, Ginger McCain, Headline 2005

The Boss, Charles Lambert, Pride of Place 1995

The Great Derbies: Everton v. Liverpool – A Celebration of the Merseyside Derby, Brian Barwick and Gerald Sinstadt, BBC Books 1988

Peter Shilton – The Autobiography, Orion 2004

The Essential History of England, Andrew Mourant and Jack Rollin, Headline 2002

Bill Beaumont – The Autobiography, Collins Willow 2003

Dalglish – My Autobiography, Kenny Dalglish, Coronet Books 1996

Gray Matters – The Autobiography, Andy Gray, Macmillan 2004

The Only Game: The Scots and World Football, Roddy Forsyth, Mainstream Publishing 1990

Jules Rimet Still Gleaming: England at the World Cup, Ken Jones, Virgin 2003

Over the Top: My Anfield Secrets, Tommy Smith, Breedon Books 1998

1966 And All That, Geoff Hurst, Headline 2001

Ghost on the Wall: The Authorised Biography of Roy Evans, Derek Dohren, Mainstream 2004

Oh Joey, Joey! – My Life of Football, Joey Jones, John Blake 2005

Liverpool Greats, Ian Hargraves, Sportsprint Publishing in Association with the Liverpool Echo 1989

Kevin Keegan – My Autobiography, Warner Books 1997

Man on the Run: An Autobiography, Mick Channon, Arthur Barker 1986

The Boot Room Boys: Inside the Anfield Boot Room, Stephen F. Kelly, Collins Willow 1999

Golden Heroes: Fifty Seasons of Footballer of the Year, Dennis Signy and Norman Giller, Chameleon 1997

SPECIAL THANKS

Liverpool Daily Post and Echo
The Football Echo
Kop Magazine
The Times
The Mirror
The Guardian
The Daily Telegraph
Holly Bennion and all at Tempus Publishing
Peter, Linda and Helen Thompson
Graham Roe and Louise

All illustrations are courtesy of Empics.

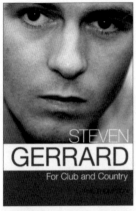

Steven Gerrard For Club and Country
PHIL THOMPSON

Skilful and aggressive, Steven Gerrard has a knack of scoring spectacular goals for club and country. Now captain of Liverpool FC, Gerrard has already led his side to Champions League glory and, having signed a new four-year contract in the summer of 2005, supporters hope his drive and dynamism will lead them on to many more successes in the future. Including a comprehensive collection of illustrations, this is the compelling story of a nation's hero.

0 7524 3793 3

The England Managers The Impossible Job
BRIAN SCOVELL

Since 1946 when Walter Winterbottom became the first England manager, the position has always attracted frenzied and critical headlines. Ramsey and Robson, arguably the most successful, weren't wanted, Don Revie deserted to Dubai, Graham Taylor had to go and Eriksson's departure was dramatically announced in the lead-up to the 2006 World Cup Finals. This look back at the men in 'the impossible job' is laced with insights and behind-the-scenes anecdotes, making it a compelling read for all football fans.

0 7524 3748 8

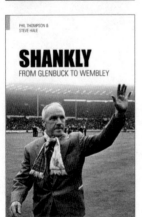

Shankly From Glenbuck to Wembley
PHIL THOMPSON & STEVE HALE

Bill Shankly is the man who shaped Liverpool Football Club. His legendary status on Merseyside and within the history of the game cannot be overstated. Having been in charge at Carlisle, Grimsby, Workington and Huddersfield, he arrived at a struggling Liverpool in 1959 and transformed the club. This delightful illustrated biography records his life – from his birth in Glenbuck to the glory days when Shankly laid the foundations for Liverpool's rise to domination of the domestic and European football scene.

0 7524 2943 4

Liverpool in the 1970s
PHIL THOMPSON

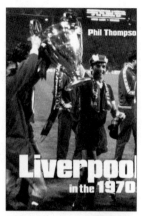

When the legendary Liverpool manager Bill Shankly retired in 1974 he was leaving in place at Anfield the second outstanding team that he had assembled. With new boss Bob Paisley at the helm, trophy after trophy found its way to Anfield, the team achieving immortality with European Cup wins in 1977 and 1978, and by the end of the decade the Reds were firmly established as one of the great clubs in world football. This book documents, in words and pictures, the sensational exploits of Liverpool in the 1970s.

0 7524 3431 4

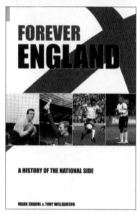

Forever England A History of the National Side
MARK SHAOUL & TONY WILLIAMSON

This insightful and fascinating account, which covers the careers of England's all-time great players and the team's successes, failures and near misses, is an essential read for anyone interested in the history of the three lions. From the amateur gentlemen of the 1870s to the stars of the early twenty-first century, with many wonderfully evocative illustrations, it is the definitive history of England's national football team.

0 7524 2939 6

Voices of '66 Memories of England's World Cup
NORMAN SHIEL

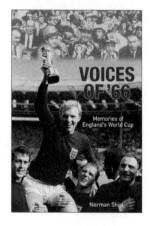

Still remembered as England's finest hour, the summer of 1966 remains for many a very special moment in their lives. By recording the recollections of people who were involved with and affected by England's World Cup, this book captures the heady days when football actually came home. Including reminiscences from fans, players, administrators and television commentator Kenneth Wolstenholme, as well as many illustrations, this book will breathe life into a vital part of England's sporting heritage.

0 7524 3929 4